P9-AOW-908

ROCKETS

Ron Miller

TFCB
Twenty-First Century Books
Minneapolis

This book is dedicated to Max and Tatum Pelczarski.

Twenty-First Century Books
A division of Lerner Publishing Group, Inc.
241 First Avenue North
Minneapolis, MN 55401 U.S.A.

Website address: www.lernerbooks.com

Library of Congress Cataloging-in-Publication Data

Miller, Ron, 1947–
Rockets / by Ron Miller.
p. cm. — (Space Innovations)
Includes bibliographical references and index.
ISBN-13: 978–0–8225–7153–7 (lib. bdg. : alk. paper)
1. Rockets (Aeronautics)—Juvenile literature. 2. Rocketry—Juvenile literature. I. Title.
TL782.5.M455 2008
621.43'56—dc22 2006021220

Manufactured in the United States of America
1 2 3 4 5 6 – DP – 13 12 11 10 09 08

CONTENTS

Introduction 5

Chapter 1
Medicine and the Fire Arrow 6

Chapter 2
The Rockets' Red Glare 16

Chapter 3
The Experimenters 30

Chapter 4
The Rocketeers 42

Chapter 5
The Rocket Grows Up 56

Chapter 6
A Rocket for Every Need 70

Chapter 7
The Future of Rockets 94

Glossary 104

Source Notes 106

Bibliography 107

For Further Information 108

Index 110

INTRODUCTION

Few human inventions are associated with the future more than rockets. They have enabled humans to escape the gravitational bonds of Earth and fly to the Moon and beyond. Rockets have placed satellites into orbit that let us view our planet from a perspective impossible from the ground. Instead of seeing no farther than the horizon around us, we can see our entire world in a single glance.

Rockets have saved the lives of shipwreck victims—and cost lives during war. Rockets will someday carry humans to Mars and other planets and allow us to mine asteroids for metals and minerals. Perhaps they will save our world from the impact of an asteroid. Rockets of one kind or another may even carry us to the stars.

Rockets have been a symbol of the future for so long that it is surprising just how old and primitive they are. Rockets are actually very simple devices. In their most basic form, they have no moving parts. In fact, other than a tube of fuel that is closed at one end, the simplest rockets might not have any parts at all. Rockets operate by the application of one of the most basic laws of nature: for every action there is an equal but opposite reaction. Rockets were probably invented by accident in China nearly two thousand years ago. That is where the story of rockets begins.

Observers in the 1950s watch the launch of one of the rockets in the Bumper series. These rockets, which consisted of a German V-2 first stage and a U.S. WAC-Corporal second stage, were the first to reach the edge of space.

1 MEDICINE AND THE FIRE ARROW

The Chinese invented rockets nearly two thousand years ago and were the first to use them in warfare. The 1950s painting by Jack Coggins *(top)* and the Chinese art below it show early rockets.

Nearly two thousand years ago—at least as early as the second century—Chinese doctors and alchemists (who experimented with chemicals) were mixing sulfur and saltpeter to create medicines that might cure ills and prolong human life. Bright yellow crystals of sulfur were easy to find, occurring naturally around volcanoes and hot springs. Saltpeter, a white, crystalline substance, was readily available too. It could be collected from the floors and walls of caves.

Saltpeter is a kind of salt formed from excrement, such as bat droppings, and decaying vegetation. Nitrogen compounds produced by the decay are dissolved by rainwater and deposited on surfaces in the form of white crystals. It is called saltpeter, or stone salt, because it is a salty substance found on or within rocks (*peter* is from the Latin word for "rock"). Raw saltpeter can be purified by boiling. This allows unwanted material to be skimmed off the top. One of the earliest uses of saltpeter may have been in the curing of meats to help prevent spoilage. In fact, saltpeter is still being used for this.

Ancient humans discovered that wood soaked in a saltpeter solution and then allowed to dry would burn much more quickly than ordinary wood. Tinder made from shredded wood or dried fungus saturated with saltpeter made an excellent and reliable fire starter. This was probably a chance discovery, made when a piece of wood used for stirring a solution of boiling saltpeter accidentally fell into a fire. Someone may have noticed that it burned faster and brighter than plain wood.

Chinese alchemists such as Chen Yuan (A.D. 220–300) were careful while heating mixtures containing saltpeter. Careless experimenters had been badly hurt and houses even burned to the ground after heating a mixture of saltpeter, realgar (arsenic sulfide), sulfur, and honey. Eventually, experimenters realized that if this mixture were ignited intentionally rather than accidentally, it was actually fun to watch it burn.

Soon someone discovered that if the quick-burning mixture of saltpeter, sulfur, and charcoal—the ingredients of gunpowder—were tightly encased in a tube of thick paper or inside a section of bamboo, it would explode with a loud bang. While gunpowder is believed to have been developed very early, the first clear references to it are found in Chinese books written between the seventh and twelfth centuries. For example, the early alchemist Ch'ing Hau-Tzu reported setting fire to a mixture containing saltpeter and sulfur.

Chinese characters representing the word *rocket*

By the tenth century, special words had been coined to describe firecrackers and fireworks. By the end of that century, fireworks had become widely popular as entertainment. Still, the earliest Chinese name for gunpowder, *huo yao*, which means "fire drug," may have reflected its original use as a medicine.

The Chinese military quickly realized the potential of the new substance. By the eleventh century, the proper proportions of the ingredients had been calculated (they were hardly different from those used in modern gunpowder). Its explosive power had become well known.

Most military applications of gunpowder were limited to launching projectiles and setting fire to enemy towns and fortifications. "Fire arrows" were widely used to "burn down the wood, straw, and catapults of the enemy." These were not rockets, however. They were usually ordinary arrows that had small explosive charges attached to their tips. Fuses were attached to these explosive charges and lit. Then the arrows were launched toward the enemy.

Rockets were most likely invented accidentally when a poorly made firecracker didn't explode and, instead, allowed a jet of gas to escape from one end. This caused the firecracker to suddenly fly forward. This was probably first used for amusement, just as fireworks were originally used.

This nineteenth-century Chinese watercolor painting shows rocket makers at work.

One popular firework was called the ground rat (*ti lao shu*). It was designed to race across the ground in an unpredictable course. A story from China's Ming dynasty tells how, in 1419, a group of visiting Persians were entertained. On Lantern Festival Day, ground rats raced around, lighting the thousands of lanterns on display.

Another story of the fiery ground rat occurred one hundred years earlier and was considerably more amusing. "During the royal banquet in the palace," reported a historian during the Southern Sung dynasty, "the Empress-Dowager was entertained by the Emperor Li-Chung with 'yen huo' fired in the court. Suddenly a 'ground rat' ran quickly to the Dowager and went beneath her chair. She was so frightened and angered, that the banquet was called off. Those responsible were put in jail, and the Emperor apologized."

The First Rockets

One of the earliest mentions of rockets in Chinese literature is in *Ching Shih* (History of the Ching Dynasty). This book, written in 1345, declares that perhaps the first practical use of the rocket was made in Kai-fung-fu in 1232. The city was under siege by Mongols, who were unpleasantly surprised by two new weapons. The first was an explosive bomb dropped from the top of the city walls. The other was called *fe-ee-ho-tsiang*, or "arrow of flying fire." These rockets carried warheads containing an

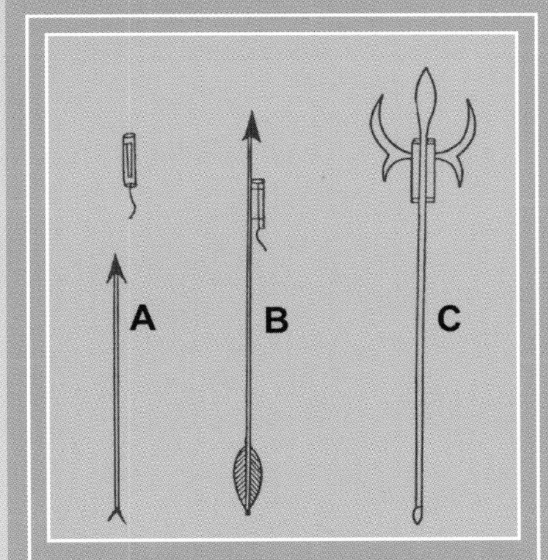

Fire arrows (*huo chien*) and a fire lance (*huo tsang*) from a seventeenth-century Chinese book: (A) a fire arrow and the incendiary device it carried, (B) a fire arrow with the incendiary device attached, (C) a fire lance with two flame ejectors attached

This 1952 watercolor painting by Jack Coggins shows the first recorded use of rockets in warfare. It occurred in A.D. 1232 at the battle of Kai-fung-fu. The city was under siege by Mongols, who were repulsed when the Chinese used rockets against them.

inflammable substance that would explode over a wide area on impact. The rocket itself must have been invented much earlier, however, for such an advanced version to be available at that date and for the Chinese soldiers to be so skilled in its use.

No one knows exactly what these first rockets looked like. They

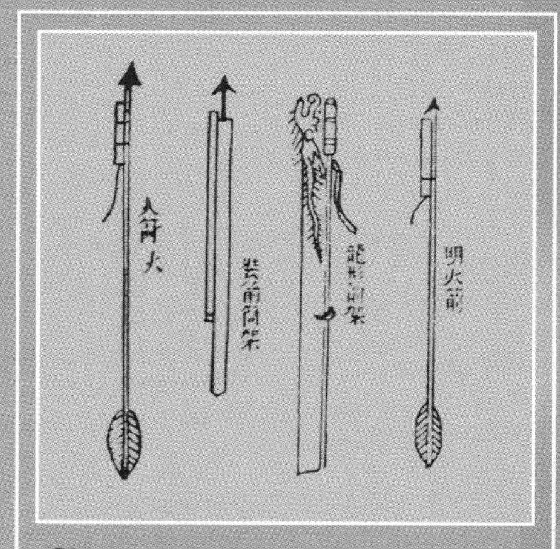

Chinese rocket arrows

were probably ordinary arrows with rockets attached, since pictures of later rockets were shown to look like this. Even as late as the beginning of the twentieth century, Chinese fireworks rockets would often have feathers attached to the ends of their sticks. This was a carryover from their ancient origins as fire arrows. (It was also a useless one too, since the exhaust of the rocket probably quickly burned away the feathers.)

Early rockets could not be aimed with any sort of accuracy. Once they were launched, they pretty much went where they pleased. But by launching hundreds all at the same time, the Chinese were assured of having at least some effect on their enemies. The sight and sound of masses of flaming rockets arching through the air and exploding everywhere must have been terrifying.

An ancient Chinese drawing shows fire arrows being launched by soldiers.

Soon the secret of the new weapon leaked out. For example, the Syrian scholar Hassan al-Rammah wrote a book in the thirteenth century that not only contained recipes for gunpowder but instructions for making rockets, as well. He called these *alsichem alkhatai*, or "Chinese arrows." Hassan's book also contained what may have been an original design by the author for a brand-new war rocket. He described it as a "self-moving and combusting egg." It consisted of a kind of flying-saucer shape with two sticks protruding from the rear rim, each with a tail on the end.

The Rocket Reaches the West

Both gunpowder and rockets had made their way to Europe even before al-Rammah wrote his book. The English monk Roger Bacon was one of the first to describe and write about them. In a book written around 1249, Bacon included instructions for making gunpowder and rockets. Yet, he used a code that kept many people from learning the secret.

Just as had occurred in China, the first use for gunpowder was amusement. The first rockets were created for elaborate fireworks displays, which quickly became popular among the royalty of Europe. So popular, in fact, that many courts appointed official royal pyrotechnicians to design and execute the displays. The Italian Ruggieri family, for instance, provided pyrotechnicans for the royal houses of Europe for many generations.

Rockets were quickly adapted by the military as warfare as early as 1258. They were used successfully in the battle for the Isle of Chiozza in Italy in 1379. One historian's description of the siege described the new weapon as a *rocchetta*. This is the Italian word for a "small spindle," which rockets resembled. The modern English word *rocket* is derived from this.

The German military engineer, Konrad Kyeser von Eichstädtt, described three types of rockets in his book *Bellifortis* (1405). He mentioned those that rise vertically like skyrockets, those that float on water, and those that run along taut strings. A book of drawings kept by the Italian engineer Joanes de Fontana contained designs for a large number of rockets. Some of these may have actually been constructed, but most probably never got off the drawing board. They included rocket cars that ran along the ground, meant to set fire to enemy fortifications, and rocket-powered torpedoes to be used against ships.

Other writers from around this time had more practical ideas. For example, Jean Froissart (who died around 1410) suggested that rockets might be more accurate if they were shot from tubes. This method is still used. Others suggested that rockets be equipped with parachutes.

By the first decades of the seventeenth century, rockets were used less by the military. The rocket was more or less relegated to playing a relatively small role—as entertaining fireworks displays. (But at sea, however, sailors used rockets for sending signals and

This image is from a book on pyrotechnics that was published in Germany in 1630. It shows a rocketeer taking aim at his target.

This French illustration depicts one of the official rocketeers belonging to the seventeenth-century court of Louis XIV of France.

pirates used them to set fire to other ships.)

But even if the military was losing interest in the rocket as a weapon in favor of the much more reliable and powerful cannon and handgun, the rocket still had its enthusiastic proponents. In 1668 Colonel Christoph Friedrich von Geissler, a commander of field artillery in Saxony (then a region of northern Germany) and Poland, conducted his own secret experiments with rockets. His rockets were very large for the time, weighing from 55 to 132 pounds (25 to 60 kilograms). They were made of wood covered with canvas soaked in glue. They were propelled by specially made gunpowder and carried a 16-pound (7 kg) warhead. The exhaust from these impressive rockets blasted a deep hole in the ground at takeoff.

Geissler published the results of his experiments in a book. It inspired a large number of people to perform their own experiments. Rockets grew ever larger and heavier, with 100-pound (45 kg) rockets being built by 1730. Experiments were also made to improve the gunpowder propellant. Many different proportions of the ingredients

This French diagram shows the art of rocket making as it was in 1747. The skyrockets of today are made with techniques not much different from those employed hundreds of years ago.

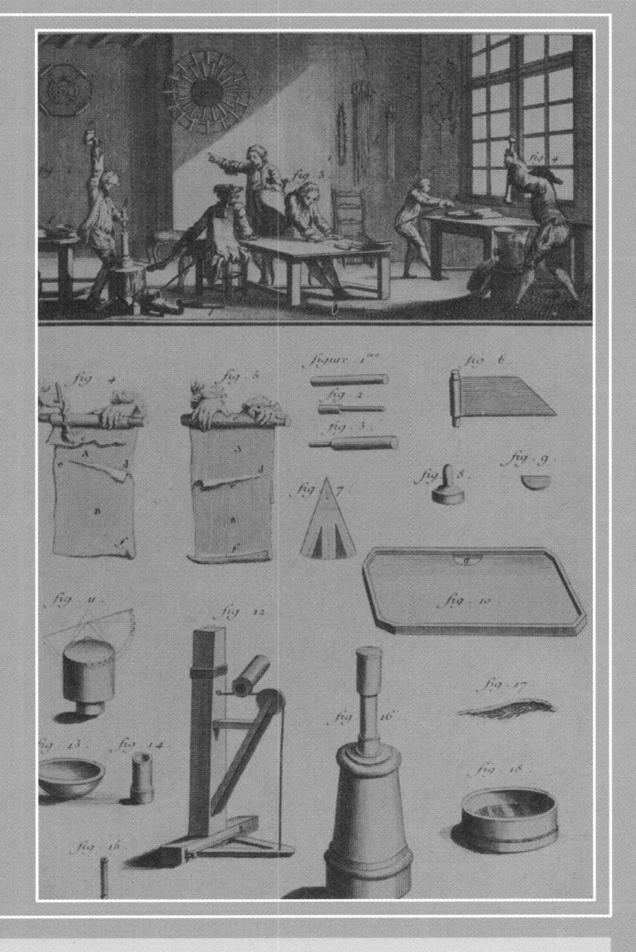

were tried. As one observer reported, “The rocket case weighed 33 lbs [15 kg], the charge 23 lbs [10 kg], the guiding stick 33 lbs [15 kg] and the cap and payload 4 lbs [1.8 kg], the whole rocket, therefore, 93 lbs [42 kg]. It rose to an extremely high altitude.”

As successful and interesting as these experiments were, they still did not convince the military that the rocket had a serious future as a weapon. It took an embarrassing military defeat to do that.

2 THE ROCKETS' RED GLARE

At the end of the eighteenth century, Great Britain was well into its efforts to colonize India. The Indian population resisted the invading British forces. In at least one battle, this resistance took an entirely unexpected form.

Prince Hydar Ali of Mysore was one of the Indian rulers who most actively resisted the British invasion. In addition to his regular army, the prince formed a company of 1,200 rocket gunners. The rockets these men launched toward their enemy were not the cardboard rockets the British were accustomed to seeing at royal fireworks displays. They were iron tubes weighing 6 to 12 pounds (2.7 to 5.4 kg), guided by 10-foot (3-meter) bamboo sticks. These could carry a warhead made from the end of a sword or sharpened stake anywhere from 1 to 1.5 miles (1.6 to 2.4 kilometers). They were not too accurate, but when hundreds were launched at once, accuracy didn't matter.

Encouraged by the success of his father's rocket corps, Hyder Ali's son Sultan Fateh Ali Tipu increased the number of men to five thousand. The British suffered severe defeats in

The British were inspired by Indian rocket troops in the early decades of the nineteenth century. In the images above, British soldiers are using William Congreve's rockets on both sea *(top and bottom)* and land *(middle)*.

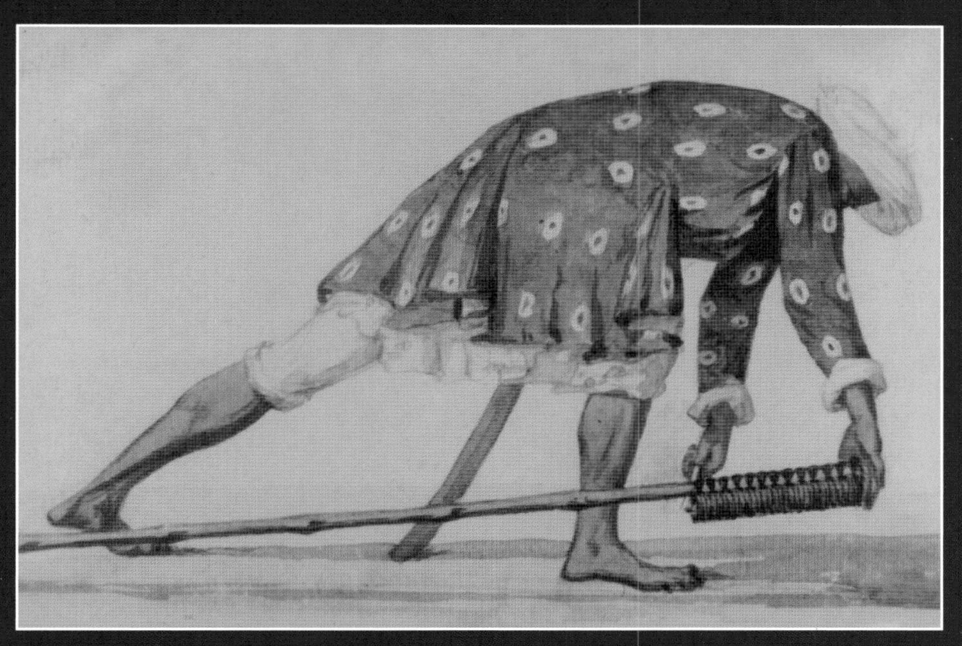

An Indian rocketeer prepares to launch his rocket. It was the effect of rockets such as this one that impressed William Congreve so much.

1792 and 1799. The British army began to reconsider its low opinion of the rocket's value as a weapon.

British colonel William Congreve immediately purchased the largest skyrockets he could find in London, paying for them himself. He began a series of tests to see just how far an existing British rocket could travel. This turned out to be about 600 yards (550 m), only half the distance of an Indian war rocket. He took this information to the Royal Laboratory at Woolwich and obtained permission to use the laboratory and its firing ranges.

Congreve soon developed a rocket capable of flying 2,000 yards (1,830 m). He demonstrated this new rocket for the prince regent. The government quickly approved rockets for the navy. The navy used them in devastating attacks against Boulogne, France, and Copenhagen, Denmark. Most of Copenhagen was burned to the ground after a barrage of hundreds of rockets.

Colonel William Congreve

Congreve's first military rockets were intended only as incendiary devices. Their sole purpose was to set fires wherever they landed. They were made of cast iron and were 3.5 inches (8.9 centimeters) wide and 40.5 inches (103 cm) long, with a 16-foot (4.8 m) guide stick attached. (In 1813 he changed the design so that instead of the guide stick being attached to the side of the rocket, the guide stick was inserted into the center of the base. The rockets were better balanced and more accurate.) By 1817 Congreve had increased the types of rockets he was producing. This included all sorts of

In 1806 the British navy used Congreve rockets in its siege of French emperor Napoleon's headquarters at Boulogne, France. More than one-third of the city was destroyed by fires started by the rockets, with only slight losses on the British side.

This contemporary illustration depicts a trained British rocket corps demonstrating the ease of launching a Congreve rocket.

explosive bombs and other devices, such as flare rockets equipped with parachutes.

Congreve was convinced that his rockets would soon replace artillery on the battlefield. They were inexpensive to manufacture, relatively easy to use, and light and easily movable. They were neither more nor less accurate than the artillery of the time. The biggest advantage of the rocket, however, was its lack of recoil.

When a gun is fired, it becomes a kind of rocket. A blast of gas is ejected from the muzzle, along with a heavy bullet. This pushes the gun in the opposite direction. Isaac Newton's third law of motion explains this phenomenon: for every action, there is an equal and opposite reaction. This backward movement of the gun is called recoil. This is merely a nuisance on land, where a cannon can be attached to a heavy carriage to absorb the shock of recoil. But on a ship at sea, it is entirely different.

The bigger and heavier a gun is, the larger the ship must be. The recoil from a big gun causes a navy ship to lurch uncontrollably.

How Rockets Work

In the late 1600s, English scientist and mathematician Isaac Newton developed laws that explained how and why things move the way they do. Although he never mentioned the rocket, the third of his three laws of motion describes how rockets work. It states that for every action there is an equal and opposite reaction. So if something is pushed forward, something else must move backward by an equal force.

When a gun is fired, the burning gunpowder forces a bullet forward from the barrel. Meanwhile, the gun moves backward, or in the opposite direction. The opposite movement is called recoil. This raises a question, however. If the opposite reaction is supposed to be equal, why doesn't the gun fly backward with the same force and speed as the bullet? The answer to this lies in Newton's second law of motion. This states that the more massive an object, the slower it is to accelerate. So it is harder to get a heavy object to move than a light one. Since the gun weighs many times more than the bullet, it reacts much less to the force.

If a gun shot out a continuous stream of bullets—as a machine gun does—the recoil would be continuous. This is what happens in a rocket. The gas molecules produced by the burning fuel act like trillions of tiny, individual bullets. As each one is ejected from the rear of the rocket, the rocket is moved in the opposite direction according to Newton's third law.

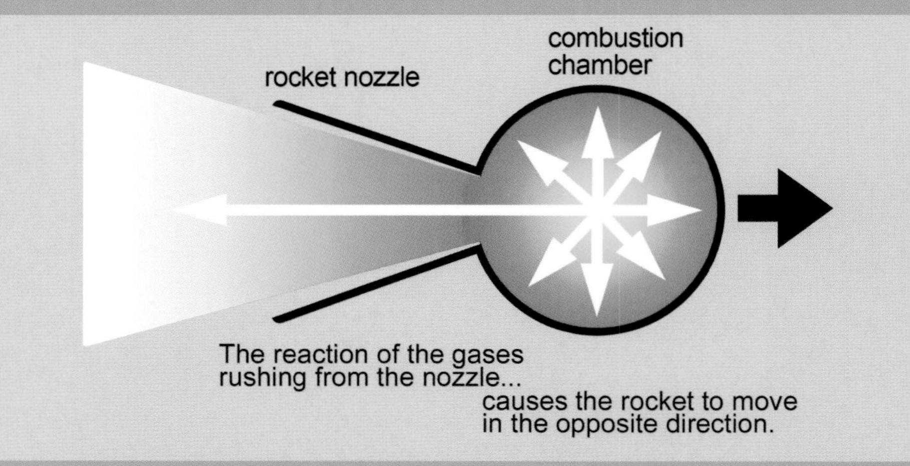

Rockets are the simplest of all motors. A fuel is burned, and the gases produced are allowed to escape from a narrow opening. The reaction of this escaping gas causes the motor to move in the opposite direction.

In this painting from the early 1800s, a British warship is firing Congreve rockets at land-based targets. The British discovered that rockets were very effective when used against cities and forts.

This is not desirable in battle. The lurching causes wear and tear to the structure of the ship. Rockets, on the other hand, require only light, thin-walled launching tubes with collapsible wooden frames to support them. Unlike a gun, the rocket is not attached to the boat in any way. In a sense, it takes its recoil with it when it takes off. The British navy realized that this meant a very small boat could carry fire-power equivalent to that of a large ship. The upstart new nation called the United States learned this very soon.

ROCKET EXPERIMENTS

You can demonstrate the principle of action-reaction many ways. The simplest way is to blow up a balloon and let it go. It will zoom around the room as the compressed air inside rushes from the mouth of the balloon (see diagram below). It will also make a funny sound.

You can create a more controlled flight by taping a soda straw to your balloon and threading a string through it. Tie the string to a pair of supports as far apart as possible. Blow up the balloon and release it at one end of the string.

You can construct a rocket car that demonstrates the principle of rocket propulsion: for every action, there is an equal and opposite reaction.

YOU NEED:
A large Styrofoam tray such as those used in the supermarket to package vegetables, 4 pins, 1 bendable drinking straw, 1 balloon, cellophane tape, scissors, compass, marker for drawing on plastic, ruler, AND measuring tape.

1. Draw the parts of your car with a ruler and compass on the Styrofoam tray. You will need a large rectangle, 4 large circles for the wheels, and 4 small circles for the hubcaps. Cut out the parts.

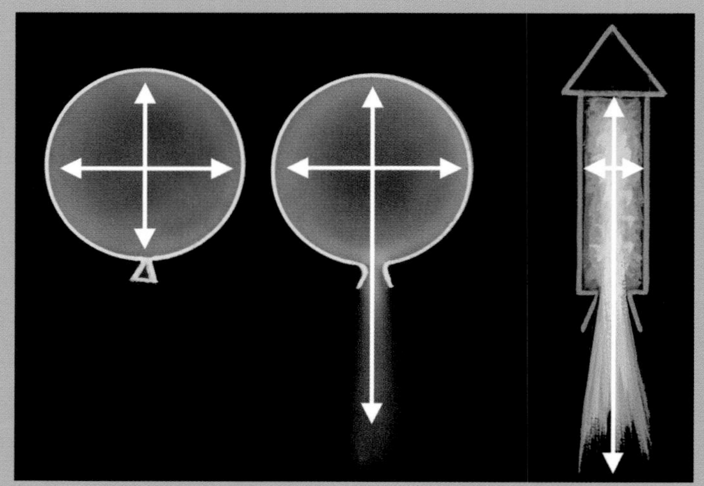

In a balloon, the inside pressure is the same in all directions. If one end of the balloon is opened, the pressure becomes unequal. The reaction of the escaping air causes the balloon to shoot in the opposite direction. The same thing occurs in a rocket: the unequal internal pressure causes the rocket to shoot in the direction opposite its exhaust.

2. Blow up the balloon, and let out the air (this will make the balloon easier to blow up next time). Pull the opening of the balloon over the short end of the straw, and fasten it in place with cellophane tape. Fasten the long end of the straw onto the rectangular Styrofoam tray, as it is in the diagram below.

3. Push the pin through the middle of the hubcaps on each corner of the Styrofoam tray.

4. Blow up the balloon through the straw. Hold the end of the straw closed by squeezing it between your thumb and forefinger, and put the car on the ground. Start your rocket car by letting go of the straw.

EXERCISES:

1. Measure the distance your car travels.

2. What can you do so that the car will go faster and farther and keep its course? Try out your suggestions, measure the distances traveled, and note the results. Which changes have the greatest effects on the results?

3. Organize a car race with your friends.

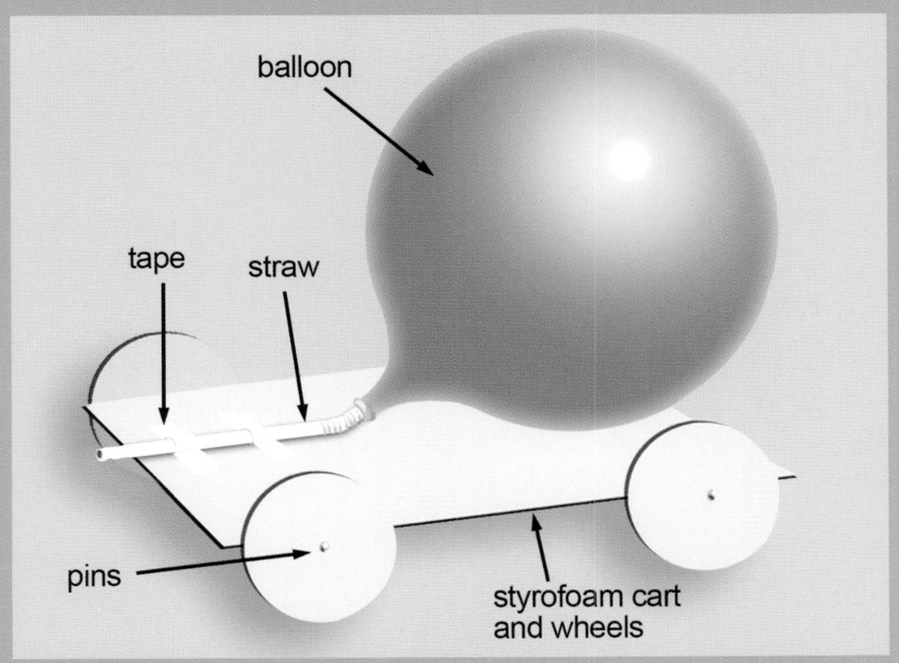

A rocket car like this one demonstrates the principle of rocket propulsion.

The War of 1812

During the War of 1812 (1812–1815), the British virtually destroyed the city of Washington, D.C., and then set their sights on Baltimore, Maryland. While Baltimore was attacked from land, ships of the British navy were poised to strike Fort McHenry and enter Baltimore Harbor. At 6:30 A.M. on September 13, 1814, these ships began a twenty-five-hour bombardment of the fort.

Congreve rockets whistled through the air and burst into flames wherever they struck. (Many of the rockets missed their targets or fell short. They landed in the waters of Chesapeake Bay, where their remains probably still lie on the bottom.) All through the night, however, the U.S. soldiers held the fort, refusing to surrender. At 7:30 on the morning of September 14, the British admiral ended the bombardment and his fleet withdrew.

Throughout that terrible night, the U.S. soldiers flew an enormous flag over the fort. They wanted to show the British invaders that they had not surrendered. Waving proudly over the fort, the banner could be seen for miles—even as far away as a ship anchored 8 miles (13 km) down the river. This is where a U.S. lawyer named Francis Scott Key had spent an anxious night watching and hoping for a sign that the city—and the nation—might be saved. He wrote a poem to describe what he had seen that night and, in doing so, immortalized Congreve's rockets:

Oh! say, can you see
  by the dawn's early light,
What so proudly we hailed
  at the twilight's last gleaming,
Whose broad stripes and bright stars,
  through the perilous fight,
O'er the ramparts we watched

When the U.S. national anthem refers to "the rockets' red glare," it is describing the British attack on Fort McHenry in 1814 *(above)*. Masses of Congreve rockets were launched from specially equipped rocket boats. The rocketeers wore heavy leather clothing to protect them from the blast of the rockets' takeoff.

were so gallantly streaming?
And the rockets' red glare,
the bombs bursting in air,
Gave proof through the night
That our flag was still there.
Oh, say, does that
star-spangled banner yet wave
O'er the land of the free
and the home of the brave?

Rocket Science

Thrust is the force that moves a rocket. It is generated by the rocket's motor, working according to Newton's third law of motion. As hot gases escape from the nozzle of the rocket, the reaction produces a force known as thrust. The more thrust a rocket has, the more it can lift and the faster it can go.

Thrust is calculated by multiplying the amount of gas being ejected per second by the speed of the gas. The more gas that is being ejected per second and the faster that gas is traveling, the greater the thrust will be. A rocket that weighs 1 ton (1 metric ton) and produces 1 ton (1 metric ton) of thrust will not go anywhere. This is because its weight and thrust balance each other exactly. Therefore, a rocket needs to have more thrust than its weight.

Another factor considered when building a rocket is mass ratio. This is the difference between the weight of the rocket when fully fueled and when empty. The greater this ratio is, the more propellant the rocket can carry and the greater its final speed will be. Most rockets have mass ratios between 6 and 20.

The Rocket's Wane

The rocket had proved itself in battle time and again. It was eventually adapted by many other countries, which formed their own rocket troops. But the rocket still had its faults. Chief among them was the long, cumbersome guide stick. The purpose of the stick was to help balance the rocket, enabling it to fly straighter than it would on its own.

Guide sticks were only partially effective, however. The entire rocket would be balanced at launch, but as its fuel was used up, its weight would change. The stick, however, never changed its weight. The balance of the entire rocket would eventually be thrown off, and it would veer off course. The long guide sticks also made the rockets difficult to transport.

A number of inventors sought to do away with the guide stick and stabilize the rocket in some other way. They had high hopes but unsatisfactory results. A British inventor named William Hale finally solved the problem by getting rid of the guide stick entirely. To stabilize his rockets, Hale inserted three curved metal vanes in the exhaust nozzle. These caused the rocket to spin rapidly when launched.

Making a projectile spin had long been recognized as the best way to achieve stability and straight flight. An arrow with its feathers set at a slight angle will spin as it flies and travel a straighter course. If a gun or cannon has spiral grooves on the inside of its barrel, the bullet or shell it fires will spin. Like the spinning arrow, it will fly straighter.

Such a bullet will also travel farther because there is less air resistance against it. The reason this works is centrifugal force. It is the same reason why a spinning top will not fall over. Newton's first law of motion states that once an object is set in motion, it will remain in motion unless acted upon by an outside force. This means that once an object is set spinning, it will resist any change in the direction of

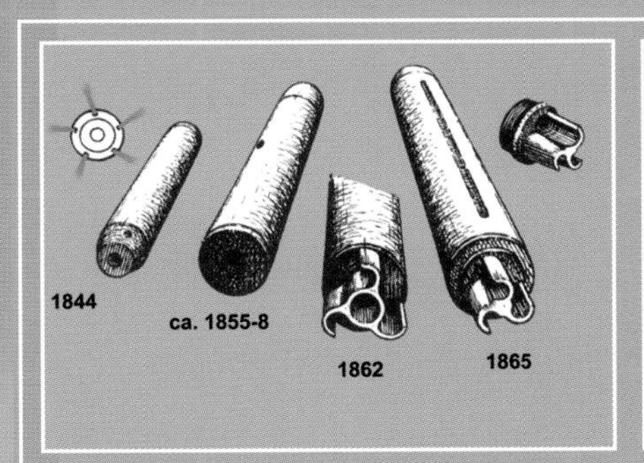

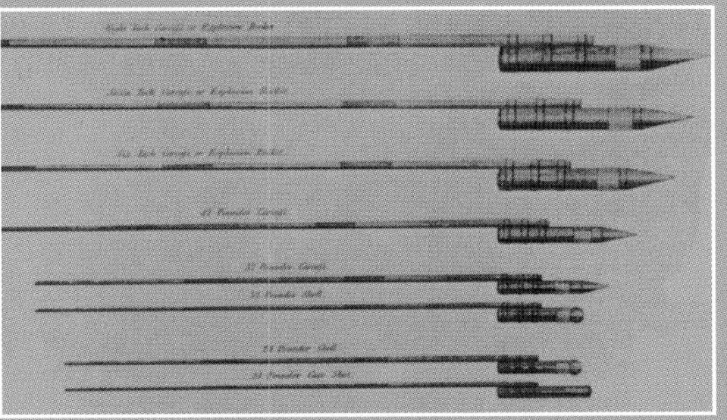

The design of the Hale rocket *(left)* went through many refinements before the final version. The idea behind the design was to impart a spin to the rocket. This would stabilize it more effectively than the long, heavy, cumbersome guide stick used by the Congreve rockets *(right)*, allowing the Hale rockets to be much more accurate.

Space Travel Enters the Scene

Rockets have long been associated with science fiction stories. After all, what is science fiction all about if not rocket ships zooming to other planets? But it is less known that science fiction authors associated rockets with space travel long before scientists and engineers did.

The first person to describe the use of rockets in space travel was the French author Jules Verne (1828–1905). In his 1865 novel *From the Earth to the Moon*, Verne describes a spaceship using rockets to change its course. Verne had realized an important fact about rockets that had escaped even most scientists: they would work in a vacuum (a space without air or gas).

Most people, including scientists and engineers, believed that rockets worked by pushing against the air behind them. This was a misconception that lasted well into the twentieth century. In fact, many of the early rocket experimenters were hampered by a lack of support from both the scientific community and the public. This is because the public didn't know that rockets don't need something to push against and

that spin. Just as a spinning top will resist being pushed over, a spinning bullet or rocket will resist being turned from its path.

Meanwhile, however, improvements to guns and cannons had increased their range and accuracy. They far exceeded the effects of rockets. Most countries began disbanding their rocket corps. By the time Hale had made his improvements, there was little interest in rockets in Europe. (A few countries, such as Russia, Austria, and France, continued to use Congreve-type rockets.)

The United States, on the other hand, had just entered its Civil War (1861–1865). This was the most technologically advanced war to that time. The Northern government showed much enthusiasm for Hale rockets. The rockets came in two sizes. The one that saw the most service was the largest: 3.3 inches (8.3 cm) in diameter with a therefore can work in the vacuum of space.

Rocket propulsion is the only type of propulsion that will work in outer space. In fact, rockets work better in a vacuum than they do in an atmosphere like Earth's. This is because air actually gets in the way of the exhaust, keeping it from achieving its full velocity.

Jules Verne (1828–1905) was one of the most popular authors of the nineteenth century and is still a best-selling author more than a century after his death.

weight of 16 pounds (7.2 kg). Made of cast iron, the rocket had a range of 2,200 yards (2,012 m). Like Congreve's rockets, the Hale rockets were launched from tubes or troughs supported by portable stands. The rockets were eventually used by the North and the South during the war.

Rockets continued to be used sporadically and unenthusiastically by armies and navies around the world for the remainder of the nineteenth century. But the U.S. Civil War was essentially the last gasp for the weapon. By then the accuracy and firepower of cannons had far exceeded the capability of the unreliable rocket, which usually had to be fired in large numbers to ensure hitting anything at all. An entirely new type of rocket was needed, but that had to wait until the dawn of the following century.

3

THE EXPERIMENTERS

Konstantin E. Tsiolkovsky was born in Russia in 1857, the son of a forester (and unsuccessful inventor) and a mother who came from a family of artisans. When he was ten years old, a bout with scarlet fever left him deaf. This made it difficult for him to attend school, so he studied at home. He read books constantly, especially books about mathematics and physics.

He did so well that in spite of his handicap, he was offered a job as a teacher at the age of nineteen. He remained a teacher, working at several different schools, until he finally retired. Tsiolkovsky never lost his interest in science and research, however. Every day, after his teaching duties had been completed, he hurried home to work on his own projects. One of these involved exploring outer space.

Tsiolkovsky knew that an ordinary motor could not propel a vehicle between planets. This is because there is no atmosphere in space (and therefore no oxygen). Steam engines and internal combustion engines require a source of oxygen. And, of course, propellers would not work in a vacuum, either. Tsiolkovsky realized that the only propulsive force that could move a

The experiments of American physicist Robert Goddard *(above)* in the early 1900s resulted in the construction and launching of the world's first liquid-fuel rocket in 1926.

Konstantin E. Tsiolkovsky, who theorized about the building of a liquid-fueled rocket in the late 1800s, published his ideas in 1903.

vehicle in space would be one that operated on the principle of recoil. And that meant rockets.

Tsiolkovsky recognized that the ordinary gunpowder rocket, which had been used for more than one thousand years, would not work. A solid-fuel rocket flies when the gases produced by burning gunpowder shoot at high speed from the rear of the rocket. Just as with anything else that burns, gunpowder requires oxygen. When you light a match, it burns because its fuel combines with oxygen in the atmosphere. Gunpowder, however, contains its own oxidizer.

Oxygen forms a large part of potassium nitrate, which readily releases some of the oxygen when heated. This oxygen is then free to combine with other materials, such as a fuel. But this system could not achieve the velocities required for space travel. A more efficient fuel was needed.

Tsiolkovsky suggested using two liquids, kerosene and liquid oxygen, for example, or liquid hydrogen and liquid oxygen. This would require an entirely new type of rocket, one that carried its fuel and oxidizer separately. The two liquids would then be forced into a small, enclosed space—a combustion chamber—and ignited. If one end of the chamber opened into a nozzle, the resulting blast of hot

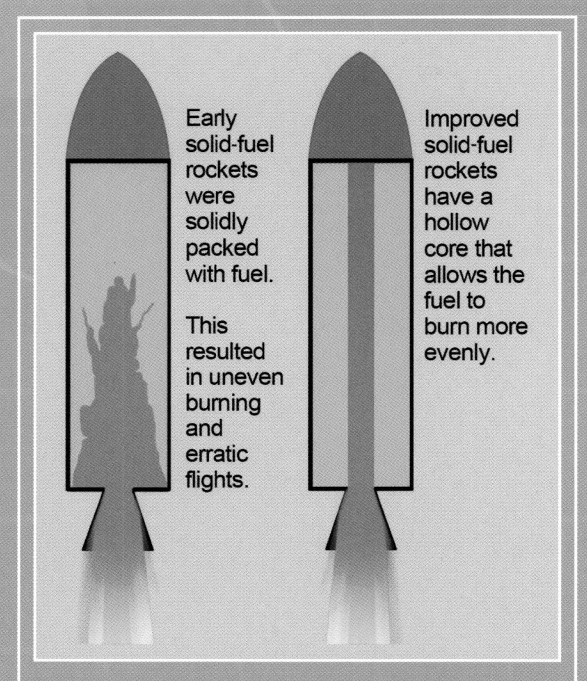

The first rockets used a solid propellant that combined fuel and oxygen. In the earliest rockets, this was gunpowder. To keep the propellant from burning irregularly *(left)*, most solid-fuel rockets have a hollow core *(right)* for more even burning.

gases would propel the rocket.

One of the advantages of the liquid-fuel rocket is that it is not only more powerful than the old solid-fuel gunpowder rocket but it can be controlled. Because the fuel and oxidizer are separated and fed into the motor, the thrust of the rocket can be adjusted by allowing more or less fuel to flow into the combustion chamber. This is similar to the way a driver adjusts the speed of an automobile by changing the amount of fuel and air reaching the engine. A liquid-fuel rocket can even be turned off and restarted. A gunpowder rocket cannot.

Tsiolkovsky finished his first paper containing his ideas regarding rockets in 1898. He submitted it to a scientific journal, and it was finally published in 1903. Unfortunately, the journal was published in Russian, a language that virtually no one outside Russia was then familiar with. Few scientists outside the country ever read Tsiolkovsky's theories. This lack of attention did not deter Tsiolkovsky, however. He persevered in his studies, producing an entire series of articles—and even a science fiction novel—outlining his thoughts about rockets and space travel. Still, all of these were published in Russian and were little known to the outside world.

Fortunately, several important events occurred in the meantime. Two other teachers—one in the United States and one in Europe—also became interested in rockets and space travel. Neither knew about Tsiolkovsky or each other. One of the teachers was Robert Hutchings Goddard, a physics professor at Clark College in Worcester, Massachusetts. The other was a quiet mathematics teacher named Hermann Julius Oberth, who lived in the mountains of Transylvania, part of modern Romania.

Robert H. Goddard

To the Moon with Professor Goddard

Robert Goddard sent a short thesis he had written about rockets to the Smithsonian Institution in Washington, D.C. The sixty-nine-page booklet, *A Method of Reaching Extreme Altitudes*, was published in 1919. In his first sentence, Goddard explained that he had been led to write the booklet as a result of his search for a method of sending scientific recording instruments to heights beyond those of balloons—or higher than 20 miles (32 km). This search, the booklet said, "led the writer to develop a theory of rocket action."

Most of the booklet discussed ways in which rockets could carry instruments into the upper atmosphere. At the end, Goddard mentioned that it would be possible for a rocket to actually carry a payload to the Moon. He speculated that a rocket could perhaps carry a quantity of flash powder (a powder containing magnesium that photographers once used to take flash pictures). This could be seen by astronomers on Earth when it exploded on impact.

Goddard came to regret that he made this prediction. While Tsiolkovsky's remarkable theories were largely overlooked, Goddard's little booklet immediately made headlines from coast to coast. His final statement about sending a rocket to the Moon was especially newsworthy.

The shy physics professor made headlines in newspapers around the country. "Modern Jules Verne Invents Rocket to Reach the Moon" shouted the *Boston American*. "Claim Moon Will Soon Be Reached," blazoned the *Milwaukee Sentinel*. "Savant Invents Rocket Which Will Reach Moon" declared *Popular Science* magazine. Of course, Goddard had not done so. He had only *suggested* that a rocket might someday reach the Moon. Goddard even received an offer from Hollywood asking if he would include a message from a popular film star in his rocket.

The worst blow came from the venerable *New York Times*. Following the headline, "Believes Rocket Can Reach the Moon," was an editorial that claimed that Goddard was simply ignorant of the basic laws of physics. Goddard's rocket, the writer asserted, simply would not work. "That Professor Goddard . . . does not know the relation of action to reaction, and of the need to have something better than a vacuum against which to react—to say that would be absurd. Of course, he only seems to lack the knowledge ladled out daily in high schools."

Criticisms such as this stung Goddard deeply. He was especially bothered by the accusation that he was capable of making a fundamental error in physics. The idea that a rocket flew by pushing against the air behind it was a common one that even many scientists believed. In fact, a rocket moves by the reaction occurring within it. It travels forward because its exhaust is traveling in the opposite direction. The faster the exhaust is ejected—the "exhaust velocity"—the faster the rocket will go.

Rather than helping make a rocket go, the presence of air actually slows it down. The air gets in the way of the exhaust. A rocket will not only work in a vacuum—as Goddard knew perfectly well—it works better in a vacuum. This public humiliation caused Goddard to retreat behind a wall of secrecy. Few people after that learned about the work he was doing.

Goddard was a skilled engineer and machinist who actually built the rockets he proposed. (Tsiolkovsky and Oberth were pure theoreticians and never actually built any of the rockets they wrote about.) Although Goddard had been talking about solid-fuel rockets in his Smithsonian booklet, he began considering the potential of liquid fuels. He wanted to design, build, and fly these rockets. But he realized perhaps more than either of the other scientists how difficult this would be.

The primary problem was how to get the oxidizer and fuel into the motor. A solid-fuel rocket, such as a skyrocket, is basically one piece—the fuel and nozzle is directly connected. The liquid-fuel rocket requires that the fuel and oxidizer be kept in separate tanks. These tanks are kept separate from the combustion chamber where the liquids are to be burned. When combustion takes place, Goddard realized, it creates tremendous pressures inside the combustion chamber. How would he be able to force liquid fuel and oxidizer into the motor against this pressure? Liquid fuels would also require plumbing, valves, and other equipment, in addition to their tanks. All would add weight to the rocket.

Goddard chose liquid oxygen for his oxidizer. After a little experimentation, he settled on gasoline for his fuel because it was

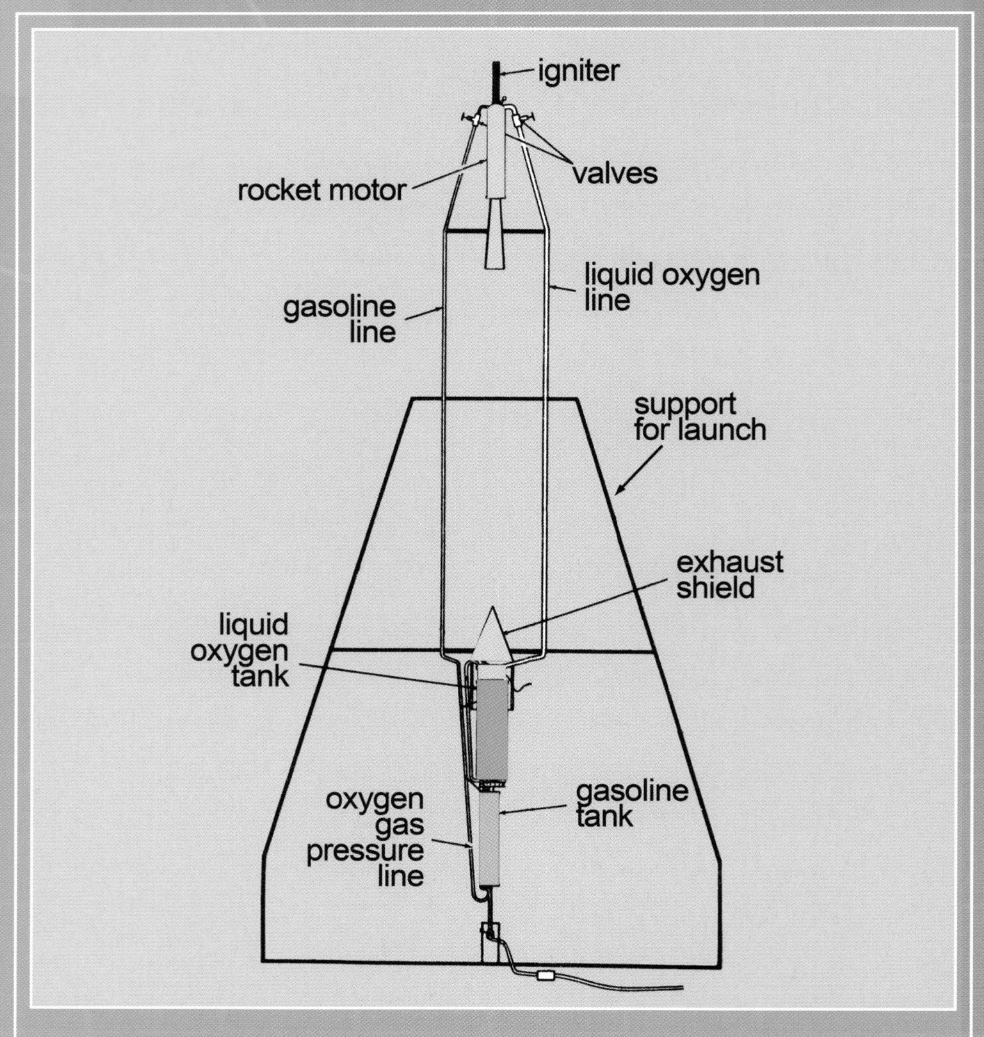

Goddard's first liquid-fuel rocket (1922) was a very simple device, hardly recognizable as a rocket. The motor was at the top, supported by the pipes carrying fuel and oxygen from the tanks below.

cheap and easy to obtain. The pressure created inside the combustion chamber by the burning fuel would be at least several hundred pounds per square inch (kg/cm). Therefore, he would have to force his oxidizer and fuel into the motor at a higher pressure.

The obvious solution would be to use pumps. At first he devised a small, high-pressure pump. But his later experiments used pressure. Goddard added an inert gas—a gas that didn't combine with the fuel or oxidizer—under high pressure to his tanks. The pressure of this gas forced the liquids into the motor.

Goddard tested his first liquid-fuel rocket motor in 1922. He was not happy with the results and began making improvements. His second motor was not ready until 1925. This motor, too, proved disappointing in its tests, so he made yet another one. Finally, in 1926, he believed that he had a motor good enough for a test flight.

On March 16, 1926, Goddard took his rocket and its launching

Robert Goddard poses beside his 1926 rocket. A few minutes later, it became the first-ever liquid-fuel rocket to fly.

frame to a snowy, open field on a farm owned by one of his relatives. He was accompanied by his wife and two men from his college. The "rocket" Goddard constructed would scarcely be recognizable in modern times. It was little more than a fragile-looking framework of

thin pipes connecting the fuel and oxidizer tanks to the motor.

Launching the rocket was simple. The fuel and oxidizer valves were opened while Goddard's assistant, holding a blowtorch attached to a short pole, held the flame under the rocket's nozzle. The motor erupted with a shrill roar, and the rocket lifted from its frame. After only two and a half seconds, its fuel exhausted, the rocket dropped back to the ground. It had traveled a distance of 184 feet (56 m) and achieved a speed of about 60 miles (97 km) per hour. This is unimpressive even by the standards of a small gunpowder skyrocket. But still, it was the flight of the world's first liquid-fuel rocket.

Unfortunately, Goddard had been badly stung by the publicity surrounding his original paper. He did not announce the successful flight of his rocket until about ten years later. Meanwhile, experimenters in Europe—unaware of what Goddard had accomplished—were making progress too.

Facing page: Henry Sacks, Goddard's assistant, ignites the motor of the first liquid-fuel rocket in 1926.

Solid Fuel vs. Liquid Fuel

All rockets operate the same way. Something is ejected from one end to make the rocket go forward in accordance with Newton's third law of motion. There is, of course, more than one way to do this. For several hundred years, rockets burned solid fuel. This created a jet of hot gas that propelled the rocket forward. Solid-fuel rockets have a number of advantages. They are extremely simple, powerful, and easy to manufacture and store. However, they cannot be easily controlled. Once a solid-fuel rocket starts to burn, it is virtually impossible to turn it off. It is also impossible to control the rate of the burning. The rocket cannot be slowed down or sped up.

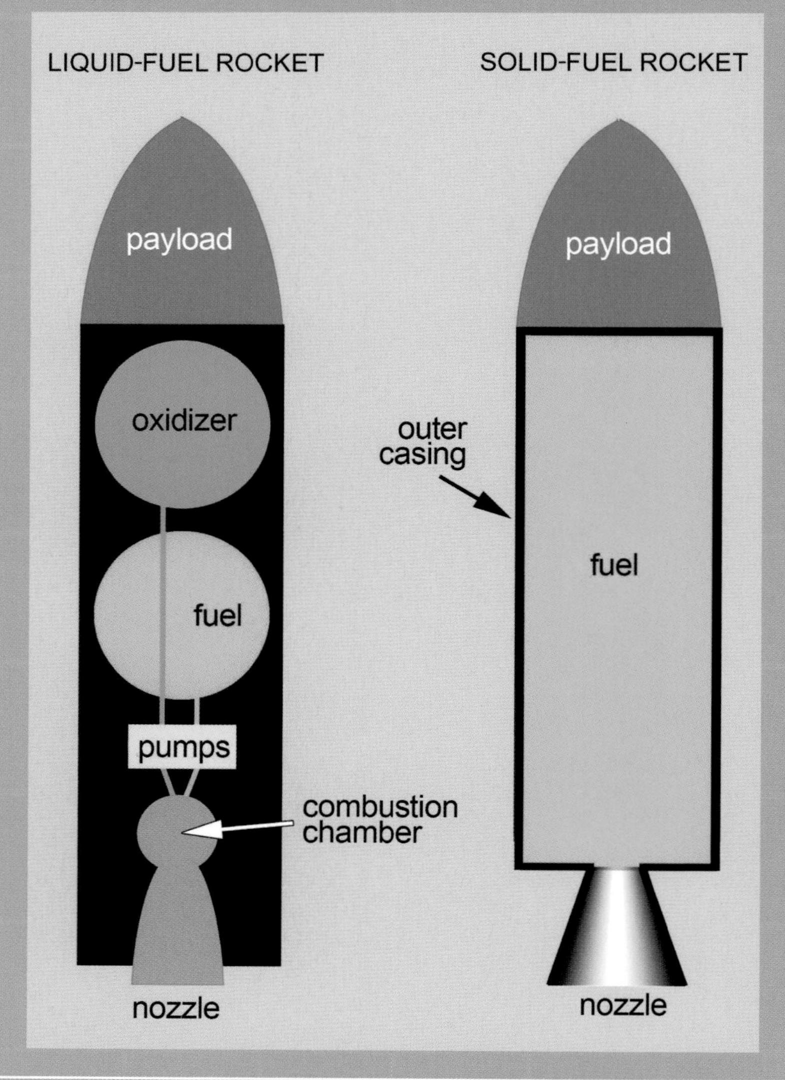

The invention of the liquid-fuel rocket changed all that. Instead of mixing its oxidizer and fuel into a solid mass, the two remain separate. They are also liquids, which can be stored in tanks. For example, most liquid-fuel rockets use liquid oxygen as their oxidizer. Almost anything that burns, such as kerosene or gasoline, can be used as a fuel.

Powerful pumps force these liquids into a part of the engine called the combust chamber. This is where they mix and are ignited. The speed of the pumps can be controlled or turned off entirely. Therefore, the rocket engine's speed can be controlled and the engine can also be started and stopped at will.

Liquid-fuel rockets are much more complex than solid-fuel rockets (since they require special fuel tanks, pumps, a specific type of motor, and so forth). But their advantages far outweigh their disadvantages, especially since liquid fuels are much more powerful—pound for pound—than solid fuels.

Facing page: The solid-fuel rocket *(right)* is extremely simple. A cylinder is packed with propellant. When the propellant is burned, the resulting gases shoot from a nozzle at one end of the rocket. Solid-fuel rockets are inexpensive and relatively simple to make, but they have several problems. The first is that solid fuels do not produce as much energy as liquid fuels. A second problem is that once it is started, a solid-fuel rocket cannot be throttled or turned off.

A liquid-fuel rocket *(left)* solves these problems—though at the expense of being much more complicated and difficult to build. Because the fuel and oxidizer are kept separate and fed into the motor by pumps or a pressurized gas, the liquid-fuel motor can be easily controlled and even turned off and restarted.

4

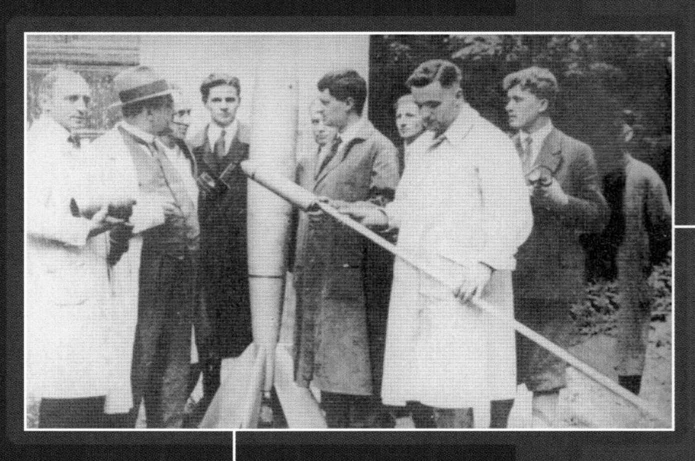

Hermann Oberth was born in 1894 in Nagyszeben in the Austro-Hungarian Empire—the modern-day small town of Sibiu, Romania. At that time, the inhabitants of Nagyszeben and many of its neighboring towns considered themselves German. Because of this German heritage, Hermann's father, a physician, decided that his son would attend the great German university at Heidelberg. There he would train to become a doctor too.

Young Hermann, however, had other ideas. He had long been fascinated by the space travel stories of Jules Verne and Kurd Lasswitz, a German science fiction writer. Instead of pursuing his medical courses, Hermann combined his interest in space travel with his interest in mathematics and physics. He started to work on a mathematical theory of space travel.

The rocket-powered vehicles *(bottom)* of Max Valier helped popularize rocketry in the 1920s. Wernher von Braun *(top and center)* was the genius behind the German rocket program of the late 1930s that resulted in the V-2.

By 1922, having completely abandoned the study of medicine, Oberth was almost ready to publish his doctoral dissertation. In it, he discussed in more detail than anyone had ever done before the possibilities of rocket flight into space. He proved mathematically that a liquid-fuel, multistage rocket could work. He described

Inspired by reading about Jules Verne's space adventures, Hermann Oberth *(left)* devoted his career to proving mathematically that space travel was a real possibility. His books were important influences in the early development of liquid-fuel rockets and multistage rockets. They also inspired many of the engineers and scientists who eventually made spaceflight a reality.

how such a rocket could be built, steered, and navigated through space. He explained how it could reenter Earth's atmosphere and be recovered. Oberth also discussed the hazards spaceflight held for humans and how people could survive in space. He even described space stations and space telescopes.

That spring, however, Oberth was shocked to read a newspaper article about Robert Goddard's booklet. He had no idea that anyone else in the world had been thinking about the same subject. He couldn't find the booklet in Heidelberg and finally wrote to Goddard, who promptly sent him a copy.

When the booklet arrived, Oberth read it eagerly. He was amazed by Goddard's ideas and calculations. But he also realized that Goddard had not gone nearly as far in his thinking as he had. Goddard had only suggested that an unmanned, solid-fuel rocket might carry an explosive charge to the Moon large enough that its flash would be visible from Earth. Oberth, on the other hand, had speculated beyond this.

Oberth realized that liquid fuels—such as gasoline and liquid oxygen—could provide twice the exhaust velocity of any powder. It was only by means of liquid-fuel rockets that the conquest of space could be accomplished. By the time Oberth read Goddard's 1919 booklet, Goddard had not only come to the same conclusion but had begun work on constructing a liquid-fuel rocket. Of course, Oberth didn't know this, especially since Goddard kept his work secret.

In 1923 Oberth published his own dissertation (which had been rejected by his college as "utopian," or impossibly idealistic). It was a ninety-two-page book called *Die Rakete zu den Planetenräumen* (The Rocket into Planetary Space). It did not sell well, mostly because Oberth's mathematics were very complex and his writing style quite technical. In fact, the publisher was so reluctant to publish the book that Oberth had to pay most of the printing costs.

Max Valier was one of the most energetic popularizers of rocketry and space travel in the years preceding World War II (1939–1945). Valier was one of the first martyrs to the dream of spaceflight. He died in 1930 when a liquid-fuel rocket motor he was working on exploded.

A writer of popular science articles named Max Valier, however, recognized the importance of Oberth's claims. Valier published a book explaining the ideas in simpler terms. The twenty-nine-year-old Oberth was amazed to discover that he had become an overnight sensation. His ideas quickly spread throughout Germany and, finally, the rest of the world. They proved that a liquid-fuel rocket was possible and that it was the key to successful spaceflight. The publisher of the original book was astonished when he had to reprint the book in an expanded edition.

But when Oberth was first writing, no one, as far as he knew, had ever built a liquid-fuel rocket. The only rockets familiar to anyone were ordinary fireworks rockets. Even the few rockets still used by the military were not much different. But a big difference existed between those rockets and the kind of rockets that Oberth proposed. For one thing, a skyrocket never moves very quickly. Almost immediately after its supply of fuel runs out, the rocket will fall back to the ground.

A liquid-fuel rocket, on the other hand, would be capable of achieving a tremendous speed. So much so that when its fuel runs out, it would keep going. It could go perhaps many times farther than it had traveled while powered by the fuel. Historian Willy Ley described the effect: When a liquid-fuel rocket is powered, say, for the first mile of its flight, it is as though it were a projectile in a gun 1 mile (1.6 km) long. The bullet from a gun will keep going for a long distance after it leaves the muzzle of the gun. In the same way, the rocket will also keep going for a long distance after its fuel is exhausted.

Oberth knew that this meant rockets were capable of reaching much greater distances than anyone had previously suspected. But Oberth went even further than proving the mathematical possibility of the liquid-fuel rocket. In the second part of his 1923 book, he outlined the characteristics of just what a high-altitude, instrument-carrying rocket would be like. In the third part, he described a manned spaceship in such detail that his readers thought they could go out and build one just by following his directions.

The Rocket Society

On June 5, 1927, a dozen German rocket enthusiasts—led by Max Valier—met in the back room of a small restaurant in Breslau in what would become Poland. All were fascinated by the possibility of using rockets to explore space. The club they founded that day was called the Verein für Raumshiffarht (VfR)—Society for Space Travel. It soon attracted some very high-profile members, although many of them joined by mail and never attended meetings.

Hermann Oberth became one of the first members. Dr. Walter Hohmann, who had written one of the first books about space travel after Oberth's, also joined. Willy Ley, who had recently written a popular book about space travel for the general public, was one of the group's founders and leaders.

Some other early members included the Russian professor Nikolai Rynin. Rynin had just published the first volume of a nine-volume history of rocketry and ideas about spaceflight. Robert Esnault-Pelterie, a French airplane manufacturer who had been giving lectures about spaceflight, also joined. Another prominent member was Guido von Pirquet, an Austrian scientist who had earlier founded the Austrian Society for Rocket Technology. Among these prestigious men were many lesser-known ones, including, by 1930, an enthusiastic teenager named Wernher von Braun.

Even as a teenager in the 1930s, Wernher von Braun had an overwhelming interest in rockets and space travel.

The fledgling society immediately ran into a stumbling block. When the members tried to register the society with the authorities, they were told that they could not. The German word *raumshiffarht*, which means "spaceship travel," could not be found in any dictionary. Therefore, it did not officially exist. They would have to change the name of their society if they wanted to register it legally. But Johannes Winkler (another founder of the VfR) argued the name couldn't be changed since it described the society exactly. Finally, it was agreed that if a definition of *raumshiffarht* were added as a footnote to the permit, the society could be registered.

German rocket experimenters gather for a meeting in 1930 (Werner von Braun stands on the far right).

Everything Rocket-Propelled

Max Valier was probably the greatest promoter of rocket flight and space travel of the first three decades of the twentieth century. He was a tireless lecturer and writer whose articles were translated and reprinted all over the world. But some of his methods for promoting rockets did not sit well with his colleagues. They considered some of his "experiments" to be little more than publicity stunts.

For example, Valier created a series of solid-fuel rocket-powered automobiles that tore around German racetracks at breakneck speeds, spewing huge clouds of smoke behind them. He also built rocket-propelled railroad cars and even a rocket-propelled ice sled. No practical use existed for such things. They were, as his colleagues thought, publicity stunts. But they served two purposes: getting the public to talk about rockets and

To show that rockets were reliable and powerful enough to use in transportation, Valier built rocket-powered cars and rocket-powered sleds in the 1920s.

Valier's rocket-boosted glider was flown by Friedrich Stamer on June 11, 1928. It was the first rocket-powered aircraft to fly. The experiment was funded by Fritz von Opel, a wealthy German car manufacturer. Later, Opel sponsored a second rocket-powered glider, the *Opel-Sander Rak 1 (above).* Piloted this time by Opel himself, it made a successful flight in 1929 but was badly damaged on landing.

showing that rockets were powerful enough and reliable enough to propel a manned vehicle.

Yet, one of Valier's experiments was important in the history of space travel. He designed and built the first rocket-propelled aircraft, which flew on June 11, 1928. It was an early, primitive ancestor of the Bell X-1—which was the first aircraft to break the sound barrier—the X-15, and the space shuttle.

The VfR immediately started publishing a journal called *Das Rakete* (The Rocket). Meanwhile, many of its members, including Max Valier, were busy giving public lectures. They were also writing articles for popular magazines.

VfR Ambitions

While educating the public about the possibilities of rockets in space travel, the VfR continued its ambition to build and launch a real liquid-fuel rocket. The members were convinced that if they could only accomplish that, some wealthy business would give them the money to build a full-sized spaceship. Because of Robert Goddard's secrecy, no one in Europe knew that he had already built and launched such a rocket. European experimenters were instead inspired by Oberth's book. It laid out all the advantages and problems of the liquid-fuel rocket in convincing mathematical detail.

Meanwhile, Johannes Winkler had gone off on his own. Employed by the Junkers aircraft company, he had been working on solid-fuel rockets to aid the takeoff of heavy aircraft. He had also privately designed a high-altitude meteorological rocket. It was intended to be propelled by a liquid-fuel motor. Backed by some private sponsors, he began work on the small liquid-fuel motor.

Winkler tested this motor on what he called a "flying test stand," which resembled a box kite. On February 21, 1931, the test stand rose to an altitude of about 30 feet (9 m). Recovered undamaged, it was launched again on March 14. This time it traveled 180 feet (55 m) high and crash-landed 570 feet (174 m) away from where it took off. This was the first flight of a liquid-fuel rocket in Europe.

The VfR was at first a little miffed that Winkler had accomplished this on his own, without informing the society of his plans. But its members were tremendously encouraged. Winkler had proven that the liquid-fuel rocket was possible.

Some of the more active members of the VfR—Rudolf Nebel, Klaus Reidel, and Wernher von Braun—had already been working on their own liquid-fuel rocket. They called it *Mirak* (for "minimum rocket"). Nebel had convinced the owners of an abandoned ammunition storage facility near Berlin to allow its free use as an experimental station. The 300 acres (122 hectares) of land containing buildings, bunkers, and blockhouses was perfect for their needs. Nebel and his colleagues posted a sign reading Raketenflugplatz Berlin (Berlin Rocket Flight Station) and went to work.

In 1931 Johannes Winkler built and flew the first European liquid-fuel rocket. This photograph shows Winkler standing with his rocket. The motor is the small cylinder at the top center of the rocket. The three large cylinders contained fuel, oxygen, and nitrogen (for pressurizing the tanks).

Nebel's immediate team included Reidel and von Braun. A separate group of buildings was run by Winkler and his assistant, Rolf Engel. Willy Ley, vice president of the VfR, used his skills as a writer to record and publicize the work. Good press was important because the experimenters had much more enthusiasm than money. They depended a great deal on Nebel's ability to talk just about anyone into giving them materials and services. The nearly penniless scientists even needed contributions of food.

The initial task was to develop a reliable liquid-fuel rocket motor. The main problem was that liquid fuels produced a great amount of heat. This tended to melt the combustion chambers and nozzles. No metals or alloys were available that could withstand such intense heat and pressure.

The obvious solution was to circulate water around the motor. This is the same way that the engine in an automobile is cooled. In 1931 the first test of the new water-cooled motor was initiated. It was successful, producing a thrust of 40 pounds (18 kg). On May 14, two months after Winkler's success, Nebel's team launched their

Eighteen-year-old Wernher von Braun *(right)* carries a Mirak rocket to its VfR launchpad outside the city of Berlin in 1930.

completed rocket *Mirak III*. It soared to a height of more than 60 feet (18 m). Willy Ley described the flight:

> The rocket took off with a wild roar. [It then] hit the roof of the building and raced up slantwise at an angle of about 70 degrees. After 2 seconds or so, it began to loop the loop, rose some more, spilled all the water out of the cooling jacket, and came down in a power dive. While it was diving, the wall of the combustion chamber—being no longer cooled—gave way in one place, and with two jets twirling it, the thing went completely crazy. [Amazingly enough, it] did not crash because the fuel happened to run out just as it pulled out of a power dive near the ground. Actually, it almost made a landing.

In spite of its wild flight, the rocket was almost undamaged. This pleased its makers immensely. Their next rocket, the *Repulsor II* (*Mirak III* was counted as *Repulsor I*), was even more successful. It rose to about the same height as *Mirak III* but traveled about 1,800 feet (549 m) horizontally. It had none of the spectacular aerobatics of the earlier rocket. Equipped with a parachute so that it could be recovered undamaged, the rocket went on to make several more successful flights. It achieved altitudes of 1,000 and 1,500 feet (305 and 457 m). Willy Ley enthusiastically reported these triumphs to the press. Soon they attracted the attention of the German military.

The Treaty of Versailles, signed at the end of World War I (1914–1918), prevented the German army from developing long-range artillery. The Ordnance Department saw rockets as a possible way to get around this restriction. In the spring of 1932, it sent three inspectors to the Raketenflugplatz. They were Captain Dr. Walter Dornberger, who was in charge of solid-fuel military rocket development; Colonel Dr. Karl Becker, chief of ballistics and ammunition; and Captain D'Aubigny von Engelbrunner von Horstig, Becker's assistant.

Working with the Army

Becker had a lifelong interest in rocketry. His interest went back to 1929 when, as a student, he helped write a textbook on ballistics. The book contained a long section on rockets. It included a description of Robert Goddard's 1919 paper and Oberth's spaceships.

When first assigned the task of developing a liquid-fuel rocket for the German army, Becker was shocked that almost no one in Germany was doing any work on them. Discovering serious experimenters was not easy. "At that time," Dornberger recalled, "rocketry was a sphere of activity beset with humbugs, charlatans and scientific cranks, and sparsely populated with men of real ability." Becker and Dornberger were not terribly impressed by the VfR's rockets. Yet, they were very much impressed by the men creating them—especially the brilliant young engineer Wernher von Braun.

The army agreed to pay VfR to develop an improved version of its rocket. The members received 1,360 marks—about $340 in modern money. In July 1932, the new rocket was tested at the army artillery range at Kummelsdorf, Germany, 60 miles (97 km) south of Berlin. The rocket reached an impressive altitude of 3,300 feet (1,006 m), but most of its flight was horizontal. It crashed about 2 miles (3.2 km) away, before its parachute could open.

Becker told Nebel that while he was unimpressed, the army was still interested in rocket development. But they had no intention of putting more money into it. Not only would the VfR have to continue its experiments on its own, Becker said, it would have to do so in secrecy. This was impossible, Nebel argued. It was only through publicity that the VfR was able to raise the money it needed. Becker replied that the army would fund further research, but all of the work would have to be done behind the guarded fence of an army base. Nebel did not like the idea of working under these conditions and refused.

Not all of the VfR rocketeers turned down Becker's offer, however. Wernher von Braun, for example, accepted an army research grant. He realized that the VfR, with its limited facilities and even less money, would never be able to develop the kind of sophisticated rocket he envisioned.

Looking back from the vantage point of the twenty-first century, it is easy to fault von Braun's decision. It ultimately led to the V-2 rocket that was so destructive in World War II. However, when the young engineer accepted the army's offer, German dictator Adolf Hitler had not yet taken power. Von Braun's acceptance was no different from that of any scientists or engineers accepting grants from their armed forces.

Wernher von Braun holds a model of the V-2 rocket he helped design in the early 1940s.

5 THE ROCKET GROWS UP

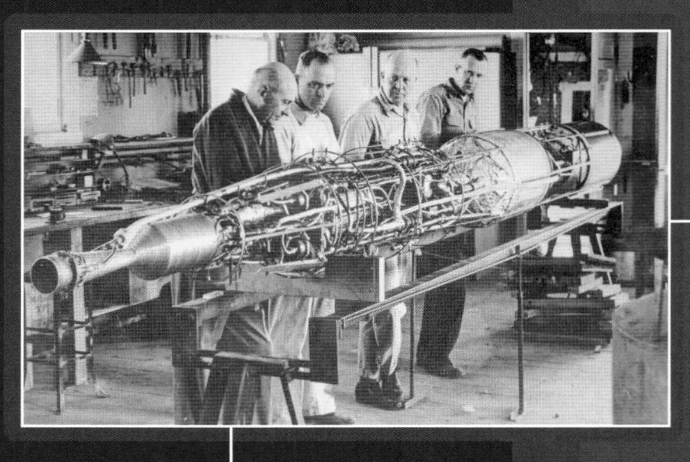

When twenty-year-old Wernher von Braun arrived at Kummelsdorf to begin his research on developing a long-range military rocket, he could not have been too impressed with the facilities. They were little better than what the penniless VfR had been working in. His "office" consisted of half a concrete bunker with a sliding roof. The other half was devoted to solid-fuel rocket research.

In spite of the poor conditions, von Braun and his assistant built a small, water-cooled rocket motor by January 1933. Fueled by alcohol and liquid oxygen, it produced an astonishing 310 pounds (141 kg) of thrust for a full sixty seconds. Six months later, von Braun had a motor that was more than twice as powerful.

This motor, instead of being cooled by being encased in a water jacket, was cooled by its own fuel. This technique, called regenerative cooling, first passes the fuel through the hollow wall of the combustion chamber. In doing so, the fuel not only carries away the heat but becomes preheated itself in the process. This motor was a great improvement. It was not only much lighter than a water-cooled motor, but the

Before World War II, the work of U.S. rocket scientist Robert Goddard *(top)* paralleled that of German engineers. After the war began, Goddard was only allowed to work on rocket-assisted takeoffs *(middle)* while Germany developed the huge V-2 rocket *(bottom)*.

A liquid-fuel rocket combines a fuel and an oxidizer in a combustion chamber where they are burned. The resulting hot gases shoot out the nozzle. The reaction to this escaping gas causes the rocket to move in the opposite direction. Liquid fuels burn at very high temperatures that would melt the combustion chamber and nozzle, so most liquid-fuel engines circulate the oxidizer or fuel through the motor walls first. This not only helps cool the motor, it preheats the fuel, making the rocket work more efficiently.

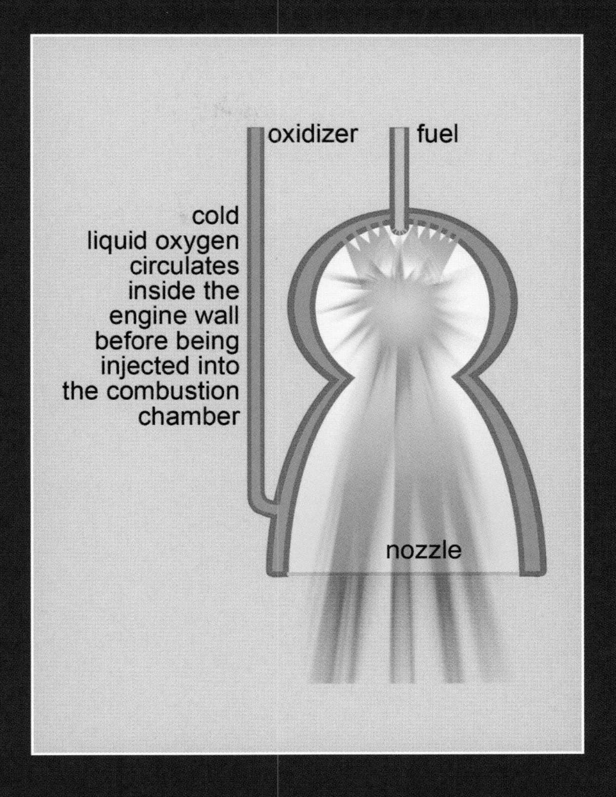

preheated fuel burned much more efficiently. Dornberger thought it was time to start building a rocket that flies.

The first attempt at a predecessor of the V-2 rocket, the A-1, failed at launch. Rather than try again, an entirely new rocket was designed. Two A-2s were tested a few days before Christmas 1934. They achieved an altitude of 1.5 miles (2.4 km). The flight of the rockets was perfectly vertical, with none of the aerobatics of the VfR rockets.

Soon other ex-VfR engineers and scientists began joining the Kummelsdorf team. An even bigger rocket, the A-3, appeared on the drawing boards. At 22 feet (6.7 m) long, it was the biggest liquid-fuel rocket they had ever tried to build. It would be propelled by a powerful alcohol-liquid oxygen engine. This would produce 3,200 pounds

Meanwhile, Back in the United States

Even though a flood of embarrassing publicity had driven Robert Goddard to retreat into secrecy, some people learned of his work and took it seriously. One of the most important was Charles A. Lindbergh. Lindbergh was a national hero who, in 1927, had been the first to fly solo across the Atlantic Ocean. Lindbergh met with Goddard. He subsequently obtained a grant of fifty thousand dollars from the Daniel and Florence Guggenheim Foundation for the Promotion of Aeronautics to finance further work.

Left to right: Daniel Guggenheim, Robert Goddard, and Charles Lindbergh in September 1935

With this money, Goddard moved his research to Roswell, New Mexico. He remained there, with a few interruptions, from 1930 to 1941. At his Roswell laboratory, Goddard created large, sophisticated rockets. He tested new, lighter metals for construction; pumps for delivering fuel to the motors; controls for guidance; and other technology. In 1935 he launched a rocket 14.8 feet (4.5 m) long to an altitude of more than 4,790 feet (1,460 m).

Goddard could not interest the U.S. military in rockets. This left Goddard, as he said, "filled with disgust at the fact that no intensive fundamental work appears possible." In 1942, after the United States had entered World

(1,453 kg) of thrust for a full forty-five seconds. In addition, it was to be fitted with many technological improvements. For example, a gyroscopic control system could steer the rocket by adjusting vanes in the exhaust.

War II, he could only get work developing rockets to boost heavily laden aircraft at takeoff. Even though Goddard's work had little direct impact on the development of rockets in Germany, Wernher von Braun admired him. In 1970, twenty-five years after Goddard's death, von Braun said, "[Goddard] was the first. He was ahead of everyone in the design, construction, and launching of liquid fuel rockets which eventually paved the way into space. When Dr. Goddard did his greatest work, all of us who were to come later in the rocket and space business were still in [diapers]."

Robert Goddard *(second from right)* and his team pose in front of one of the large Roswell rockets in the early 1930s.

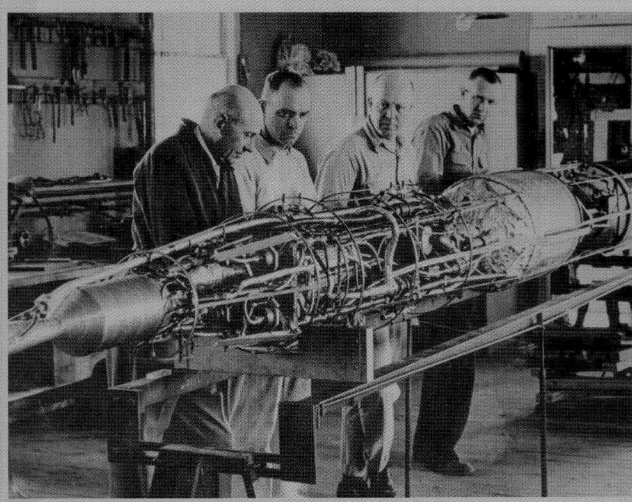

Goddard *(on the left)* working in his Roswell workshop in 1940

Unfortunately, this sophisticated system was the rocket's undoing. While the A-3's engine and other systems performed perfectly, every test ended in a crash. The gyroscopic control had to be completely redesigned. The engineers redesigned much of the rest of the

Steering Rockets

Making rockets go in a certain direction had been a problem from the beginning. The early Chinese, Indian, and Congreve rockets used guide sticks, which were not very effective. Hale and others stabilized their rockets by making them spin like bullets. This made the rocket fly straight, but there was still no way to guide or correct its flight once it was launched.

In the 1930s, Goddard and Wernher von Braun used a gyroscope to detect changes in the course of their large rockets. Basically, a gyroscope is a rapidly spinning wheel or disk. This wheel resists any attempts to change the direction in which its axis is pointing. For example, the reason a standing bicycle will easily fall over, while one that is moving

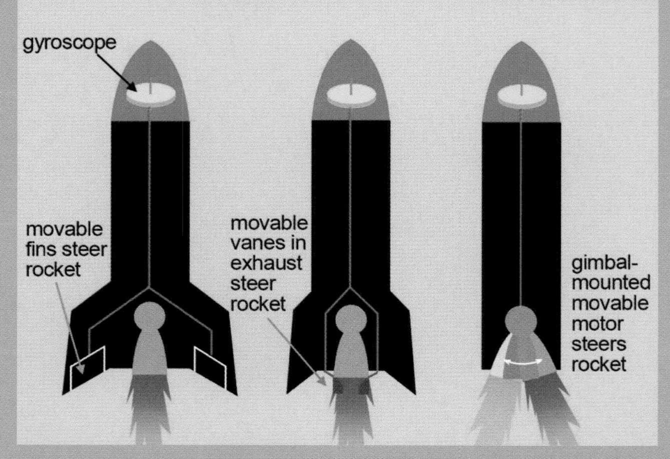

A gyroscope can be used to guide a rocket in several ways. It can operate flaps on the fins of the rocket or vanes placed in the exhaust. It can also cause the engine itself to pivot in a special mounting called a gimbal.

rocket, as well. Because the designation A-4 had been reserved for the final, perfected rocket, the revamped A-3 became the A-5. It was a resounding success. During the next two years, nearly twenty-five were launched. Some of them made repeat flights after successful parachute recoveries.

The German air force, the Luftwaffe, was impressed by this progress and anxious to expand the work of the rocket team. It moved

The gyroscope in this 1930s Goddard rocket *(left)* helped keep it on a straight course by operating movable vanes *(right)* in the rocket's exhaust.

does not, is because of the gyroscopic action created by its spinning wheels. This resistance can be made to operate controls. If the gyroscope is in a rocket, these controls can operate a steering mechanism. In this way, if the rocket veers off its course, the gyroscope can make a correction.

This correction can be implemented in several different ways. Fins can adjust the rocket's flight. Or vanes can be placed in the exhaust itself. When the vanes move, they redirect the exhaust in one direction or another. This causes the rocket's course to change. The motor can be placed in a special pivoted mount called a gimbal that allows the motor to pivot in any direction. This steers the rocket in much the same way an outboard motor steers a boat.

von Braun and his colleagues to a new facility being built near the Baltic fishing village of Peenemunde, Germany. Dornberger, promoted to full colonel, was in charge.

However, the Luftwaffe wanted a rocket that did more than just fly 10 miles (16 km). Large cannons could already fire a shell that far. The Luftwaffe informed Dornberger that if he wanted its continued support, his team would have to concentrate on creating a weapon that "could carry more payload than any shell presently in our artillery [and] . . . farther than the maximum range of a gun."

Engineers calculated that the successful A-5 could be scaled up to the largest size that would still fit through a railroad tunnel (so it could be transported). The result would be a monster rocket 46 feet (14 m) long, 5.2 feet (1.6 m) in diameter, and 26,000 pounds (11,800 kg) when fully fueled. It could carry a payload of 1 ton (1 metric ton). It would be the biggest rocket ever built.

Fuel and oxidizer would need to be pumped into the mammoth 55,000-pound (25,000 kg) thrust engine. Previously, the fuel and oxidizer tanks of most rockets were pressurized. They used a gas such as nitrogen to force the liquid into the combustion chamber. But gas pressure would not be sufficient to feed fuel fast enough to the giant A-4 engine.

The A-4 would use turbine-driven pumps. Von Braun was delighted to discover that lightweight powerful pumps already existed for fire engines. The power for the turbine would come from the steam produced when hydrogen peroxide (H_2O_2) decomposes on contact with potassium permanganate ($KMnO_4$).

Von Braun and his team were pushing known technology and engineering to the limits with their new rocket. No rocket this large or this complex had ever before been attempted. The first attempt to launch an A-4 occurred in spring 1942 and failed. The second test also failed. However, on the third try, on October 3, 1942, the giant rocket lifted flawlessly from its launchpad. It accelerated to a speed of 3,000 miles (4,830 km) per hour and rose to an altitude of 52 miles (84 km). This was really the fringe of outer space, which starts at about 50 miles (80 km). The rocket crashed to Earth 116 miles (187 km) from its launch point.

Peenemunde scientists insisted that the A-4 was not ready for field use. But the German army immediately began deploying the giant rocket. Renamed V-2 (Vengeance Weapon 2), thousands were launched

A German V-2 missile takes off during World War II.

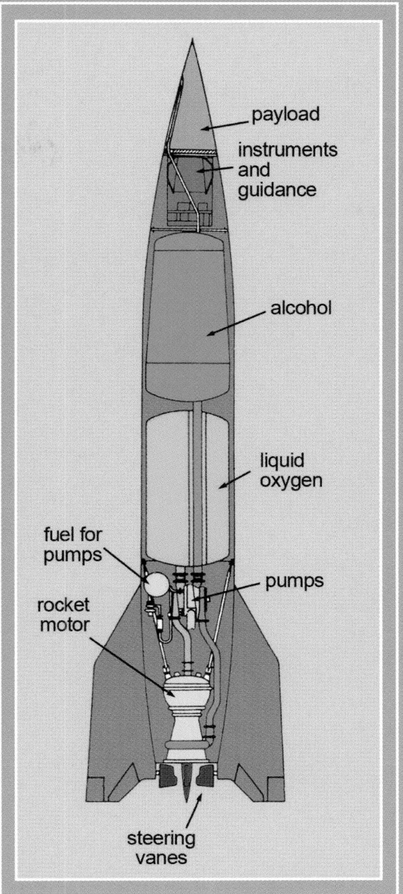

The V-2 was the largest, most complex rocket built up to its time. It was a liquid-fuel rocket burning kerosene and liquid oxygen. Powerful pumps forced these liquids into the motor. It could carry 1 ton (1 metric ton) of high explosives as its payload.

against British and Belgian targets during World War II.

The Descendants of the V-2

At the end of World War II, the United States acquired 118 of the best German rocket scientists and engineers, including von Braun. It also obtained one hundred fully functional V-2 rockets, rocket components, and literally tons of documents. The U.S. military had been anxious to get hold of the people and material because the Soviets also wanted to learn the secrets of German rocket development. Although the

Top rocket scientist Wernher von Braun *(center, with broken arm)* came to the United States from Germany at the end of World War II. He eventually led the U.S. missile program.

United States had gone into war reluctant to do any research into large rockets, the V-2 had shown the potential of rockets in future wars.

Robert Goddard—who died on August 10, 1945—examined one of these captured rockets. It was a terrible shock to the man whose pioneering work had been overlooked by the U.S. government. "I don't think he

Robert Goddard prepares to test a bazooka-type weapon he developed for the U.S. military in 1918. A small, solid-fuel rocket is inserted in one end of a hollow launching tube. The tube helps aim the rocket toward its target and helps protect the rocketeer launching it from the blast at takeoff.

ever got over the V-2," a friend observed. "He felt the Germans had copied his work and that he could have produced a bigger, better and less expensive rocket, if only the United States had accepted the long-range rocket."

Goddard was both right and wrong. The U.S. military had shown little interest in large-scale rockets during the war. Almost all the rockets used by U.S. forces were small, solid-fuel rockets, such as those used in the bazooka or some of the JATO (jet-assisted takeoff) units. These were used only to boost heavy aircraft at takeoff. On the other hand, Goddard had his own desire for secrecy to blame. Too few people knew of his work, either in the United States or abroad.

The U.S. Army decided to catch up. Between 1946 and 1951, sixty-seven captured V-2s were launched—mostly at the army's White Sands

In one of the first U.S. experiments with JATO in 1941, a small Ercoupe plane, piloted by Lt. Homer A. Boushey, was boosted into the air by twelve solid-fuel rockets with 50 pounds (23 kg) of thrust each.

Proving Grounds in New Mexico. Ironically, this was only about 130 miles (209 km) from Roswell, where Goddard had performed his experiments.

Part of the army's experimental program was the Project Bumper. This involved the launch of two-stage rockets. These consisted of a V-2 with a smaller rocket, the WAC-Corporal, in its nose. On February 24, 1949, the WAC-Corporal became the first man-made object known to reach outer space.

The V-2, carrying the tiny WAC-Corporal, reached an altitude of 20 miles (32 km) and a velocity of almost 1 mile (1.6 km) per second. The motor of the smaller WAC-Corporal then ignited, adding its speed to that already gained by the V-2. By the time the WAC-Corporal ran out of fuel, it had accelerated to 1.4 miles (2.3 km) per second.

The V-2, meanwhile, continued to coast upward, reaching an altitude of 100 miles (161 km) before finally falling back to the desert.

The first launch of Project Bumper, in which a captured German V-2 rocket is carrying a smaller WAC-Corporal in its nose, took place in 1949.

Multistage Rockets

As a rocket travels, its fuel and oxidizer tanks will empty. Since the empty tanks are of no use, their extra weight only holds back the rocket. If it were possible to cut away the empty part of the fuel tanks as they drain, the rocket would be lighter and could go higher and faster. This is what happens in a staged rocket. But instead of literally cutting away the empty parts of a rocket, engineers stack one rocket on top of another. Each rocket is called a stage.

In a multistage rocket, the first stage is the largest. This is because it must lift itself from the surface of Earth as well as lift all the stages above it. Once its fuel and oxidizer are used up, it is dropped and the next stage can start its engines. The second stage can be smaller than the first one because it only has to lift itself and the stages it carries. And as before, once its fuel and oxidizer are used up, it can be cast off. Each time an empty stage is dropped, the rocket becomes lighter and can go higher and faster. Stages can be stacked one atop the other, as in the *Saturn V.* They can also be mounted side by side, as on the space shuttle.

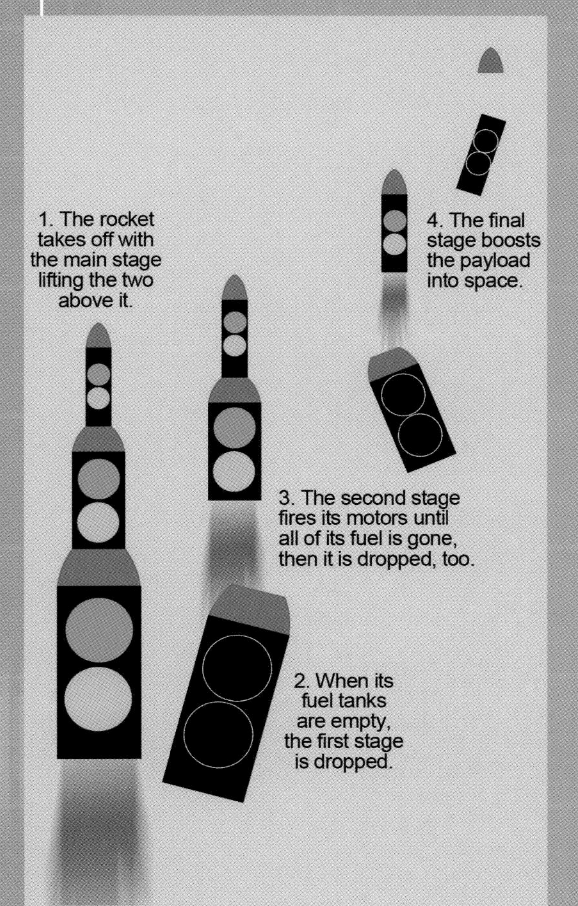

By discarding empty fuel tanks as it goes, the staged rocket *(left)* is able to travel much farther and faster than a single-stage rocket of the same size.

Although the U.S. Army Redstone missile *(above)* had been developed for military use in the 1950s, it played an essential role in the early U.S. space program. Versions of the rocket were used to launch the first U.S. satellite in 1958 and the first American into space in 1961.

When it hit, five minutes after takeoff, the WAC-Corporal was still climbing. It finally reached its peak altitude six-and-a-half minutes after launch and 244 miles (393 km) above the ground. It had reached outer space. By comparison, modern space shuttles typically orbit between 150 and 250 miles (240 and 400 km) above the planet.

By 1950 the U.S. V-2 was 5 feet (1.5 m) longer than the original and could carry five times the payload. The U.S. Army moved its rocket development to the Redstone Arsenal in Huntsville, Alabama. This is where the Army Ballistic Missile Agency was created. The Redstone of 1952 was the first large-scale U.S. rocket to evolve from V-2 technology. The Redstone was developed as a medium-range missile. Its most important role, however, was the part the 69-foot (21 m) rocket was to play in the beginnings of the U.S. space program.

The Jupiter-C, an improved version of the Redstone, launched the first U.S. satellite, *Explorer 1*. The Redstone Mercury launched the first U.S. astronaut into space. The Jupiter-C eventually evolved into the Juno satellite launch vehicle. This launched *Pioneer 3*, the satellite that discovered the Van Allen Radiation Belt that surrounds Earth.

The United States was in a hurry to develop large-scale missiles after World War II. This is because the Soviet Union had acquired a number of German rocket scientists. While most of these scientists were not as capable as Wernher von Braun and his colleagues, they were still quite knowledgeable. The U.S. military knew that the Soviet Union was using the talents of these scientists to develop rockets able to reach the United States.

The United States tended to create an entirely new rocket for every special purpose. The Soviets, on the other hand, took a more evolutionary tack. They expanded upon and improved the V-2.

By 1950 advanced models were produced at an abandoned aircraft factory. The Soviets made two major improvements. They made the payload separable from the body of the rocket. They also constructed the shell of the rocket as a monocoque. Instead of having tanks for the liquid oxygen and fuel that were separate from the rocket, the skin of the rocket was the outside wall of the tanks. This saved an enormous amount of weight, allowing the rocket to achieve greater speeds and higher altitudes. The Soviet V-2, "stretched" and modified, became larger and more powerful with each improvement. It continued to be used up to the 1960s.

The Jupiter-C rocket takes off in January 1958, carrying *Explorer 1*, the United States's first artificial satellite.

6 A ROCKET FOR EVERY NEED

Rockets were put to an amazingly wide variety of uses during the half century that followed World War II. Because of the Cold War (political and military tension between the Soviet Union and the United States lasting from 1945 until 1991), militaries were the most active in rocket development. The United States feared that the Soviet Union might be building missiles capable of carrying nuclear warheads (intercontinental ballistic missiles, or ICBMs) to the United States. This drove the United States to develop a series of large, high-powered rockets quickly. New types of rockets that use neither liquid nor solid fuels were also developed during this time.

While the U.S. Army developed the Redstone and Jupiter missiles, the navy was especially interested in large missiles that could be fired from the decks of ships and from

Top: Gloria, the first rocket-powered mail plane, is being prepared for its maiden flight in the United States in 1936. Sponsored by a wealthy U.S. stamp collector, the rocket was stuffed with letters specially postmarked to commemorate the flight. *Middle:* The mail rocket takes off over a frozen lake. *Bottom:* This is the special cancellation stamp used for the first American Mailrocket Flight.

A navy Viking rocket ready for takeoff in the late 1950s

underwater by submarines. This led to the Polaris and Poseidon missiles and the Viking sounding rocket.

Meanwhile, the air force developed its Atlas and Titan ICBMs. Although they were designed for war, rockets such as the Jupiter, Atlas, and Titan were never launched against an enemy. Instead, they played an important role in the history of peaceful space exploration.

Launch Vehicles

Launch vehicles are rockets that are designed to boost something else into space, such as another rocket, a satellite, or a space probe. They usually are not designed to carry any one particular payload. They can actually be adapted to carry a wide variety of payloads, making them very versatile, useful rockets.

Since the mid-1950s, the United States, the Soviet Union, France, and several other nations have produced a variety of launch

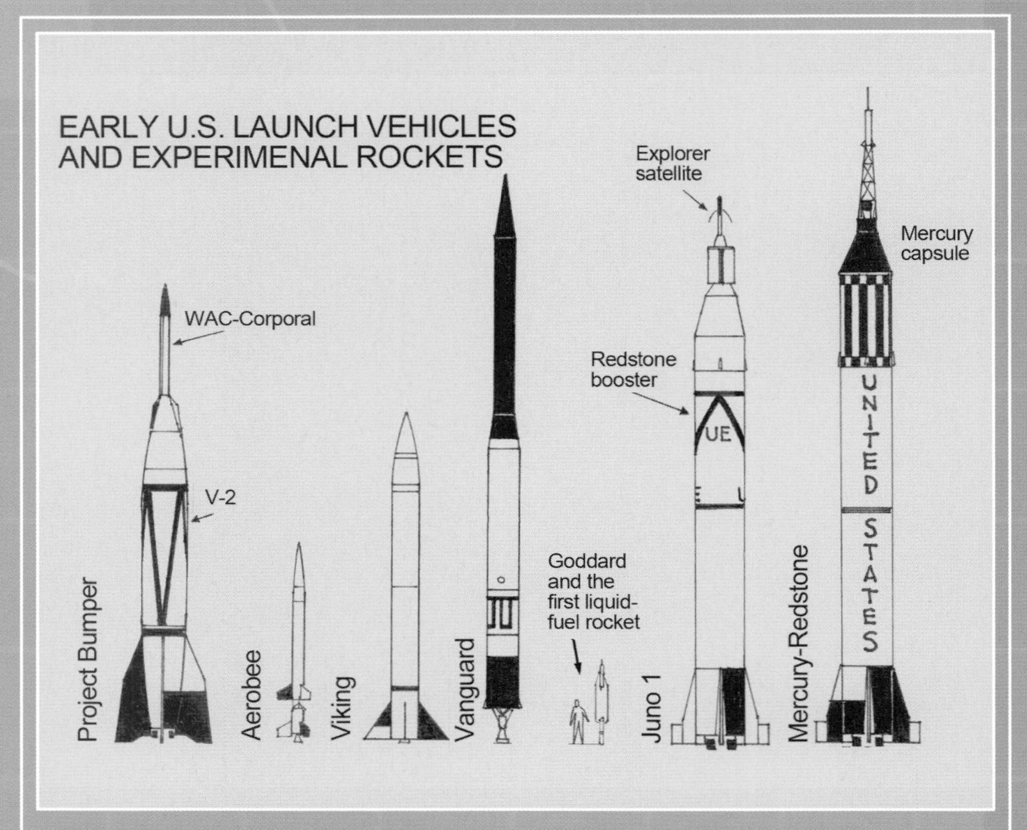

These are some of the launch vehicles used by the United States in the early years of space exploration, compared with Robert Goddard's first liquid-fuel rocket. *Left to right:* The Project Bumper rocket consisted of two stages: a German V-2 and a WAC-Corporal. The Aerobee was a highly successful sounding rocket developed in the 1950s. The Viking was a research rocket developed by the U.S. Navy, and the first stage of the Vanguard was evolved from the Viking. The Vanguard was supposed to have launched the first U.S. satellite, but technical problems delayed success and the army's Juno 1 placed the first U.S. satellite into orbit instead. The Mercury-Redstone booster was not only used to launch the first U.S. satellite, it also put the first U.S. astronaut in space as part of the Mercury program.

vehicles. Many of the earliest U.S. launch vehicles were based on rockets originally developed as military ballistic missiles. The Jupiter-C, for example, placed the first U.S. satellite into orbit in 1958. The Atlas propelled the first U.S. astronaut into Earth orbit in 1962 as part of the Mercury program. A modified air force Titan II launched the spacecraft of the Gemini program that ran from 1964 to 1966.

A larger, more powerful version of the Titan was later used to place heavy satellites in orbit. This included many of the satellites that make things such as international communication and satellite television possible. Titan launch vehicles also propelled the two Viking probes to the planet Mars and the two Voyager probes to the outer solar system.

One of the workhorses of the U.S. fleet of launch vehicles has been the Delta rocket. The first Delta was 8 feet (2.4 m) in diameter and stood 91 feet (28 m) high. Originally called the *Thor-Delta,* its first successful launch put a satellite called *Echo 1* into orbit. *Echo 1* was little more than an enormous silver balloon. It was used to

A converted Atlas missile takes off on February 20, 1962, carrying John Glenn on his historic flight into space as the first U.S. astronaut in orbit.

A Titan rocket boosts a two-man Gemini capsule into orbit. Ten Gemini flights took place between April 8, 1964, and November 11, 1966.

One of the highly successful Delta launch vehicles takes off from the Kennedy Space Center. The rocket—in many different versions—has placed hundreds of satellites into orbit and is still being used.

reflect radio signals from one place on Earth to another.

During the next three decades, thirteen more Delta-type rockets were built. The first of these could place a 100-pound (45 kg) satellite into a low Earth orbit—about 124 to 726 miles (200 to 1,170 km) above Earth. The final Delta I model was able to place a 2,292-pound (1,041 kg) satellite into orbit at 22,236 miles (35,785 km) above Earth's surface.

Delta rockets have carried hundreds of satellites into orbit. These satellites help people all over the world to communicate, predict the weather, and perform scientific investigations. The Delta III rocket can lift 8,400 pounds (3,814 kg) into orbit, which is more than twice the capacity of the Delta II.

The Scout, a low-cost launch vehicle, was first used in the 1960s. It was originally designed to place 132-pound (60 kg) satellites into 300-mile (483 km) orbits. But the three-stage, 72-foot-long (22 m) Scout gradually evolved into a larger, more powerful, and more useful rocket. Scouts have launched more than one hundred satellites, including many built outside the United States. Eventually, Scout rockets were capable of carrying 460-pound (209 kg) satellites to an orbit 300 miles (483 km) above Earth. Most of these were scientific satellites that measured such things as the

A Scout rocket is a relatively small 82-foot (25-m) four-stage rocket that is used to place small satellites into orbit. Unlike most other satellite launchers, the Scout is a solid-fuel rocket. Since introducing the rocket in 1960, the National Aeronautics and Space Administration (NASA) carried out more than one hundred Scout launches. Most of them placed satellites in Earth orbit for scientists, the U.S. Department of Defense, and customers from other nations. The last Scout was launched in 1994.

The Saturn V *Apollo* rocket of the 1960s was the largest, most powerful rocket ever made. Unlike most other launch vehicles, the Saturn V was built for a single purpose: sending a manned U.S. spacecraft to the Moon.

composition and density of Earth's upper atmosphere.

The largest and most powerful launch vehicle ever built was the monster Saturn V, which boosted the *Apollo* spacecraft to the Moon in 1969. It stood 363 feet (111 m) tall—almost forty stories. Fully fueled and loaded, it weighed more than 6 million pounds (2.7 million kg). Its cluster of five enormous first-stage engines could produce 7.5 million pounds (3.4 million kg) of thrust.

To assemble such a large rocket, scientists constructed one of the world's largest buildings, the enormous Vehicle Assembly Building (still part of the space shuttle program). Unlike most other launch vehicles, the Saturn V was designed for one particular type of mission: boosting spacecraft to the Moon.

The stages of the giant Saturn V rocket were stacked together inside the enormous Vehicle Assembly Building (VAB), one of the largest buildings ever constructed. Here, the Saturn V is being moved from the VAB (located at the Kennedy Space Center in Florida) to its launch site.

For more than thirty years, the Soviets relied on the R-7 to boost most of their satellites into orbit. In the 1960s, the Soviets also began to use the Proton to place heavy satellite loads into Earth orbit. The Proton rockets ranged from 171 to 195 feet (52 to 59 m) high and were about 30 feet (9 m) in diameter. In recent years, the Proton has also launched satellites for other nations.

The United States and the Soviet Union weren't the only countries that wanted to send vehicles into space. Many European nations were anxious to develop their own launch vehicles. This was mainly because both the United States and the Soviet Union were charging other countries high fees to launch satellites. Any country that could

The Ariane launch vehicle sits at its launch site in French Guiana, South America.

develop its own rockets could share in the profitable launch market.

Few countries possess the financial and industrial resources of the United States or the former Soviet Union. So a group of European countries including Belgium, Britain, France, Germany, Italy, and the Netherlands banded together in 1964 to form the European Launcher Development Organization (ELDO), headquartered in Paris, France. The group's first spacecraft was the *Europa 1*. It consisted of three stages. The first was a British Blue Streak missile, the second a French Coralie rocket, and the third a German Astris. Unfortunately, the *Europa 1* failed in the first attempt to launch it in 1970.

In 1974 ELDO merged with the European Space Research Organization to form the European Space Agency (ESA). The ESA-developed Ariane launch vehicle made its first flight in 1979. It began commercial service in 1984 when the first private U.S. satellite was launched on a non-U.S. launch vehicle. By the end of 2006, Ariane rockets had boosted a total of 290 satellites into orbit.

The Sounding Rocket

The earliest pioneers envisioned many uses for rockets. One, for example, included exploring the conditions of the upper atmosphere beyond the reach of high-altitude balloons. This is known as sounding. It was, in fact, the original purpose of Goddard's research.

Many of the captured V-2s launched by the United States gathered data on the upper atmosphere. Meanwhile, scientists and engineers were able to study the workings of the large rockets. Soviet scientists, too, took advantage of the military development of their own captured V-2 rockets by conducting nonmilitary research. The instruments they carried were mostly only riding piggyback during launches that were really intended for gathering information about the rocket. Consequently, larger, more efficient rockets could be developed.

The first U.S. rocket designed specifically for sounding the upper atmosphere was the WAC-Corporal. Originally conceived in 1936 by Frank Malina, it was developed in 1945 by Aerojet. This was a small company founded only three years earlier as an offshoot of the Jet Propulsion Laboratory (a research organization founded by the University of California and later operated by NASA).

The relatively small WAC-Corporal was 24 feet (7 m) long and 1 foot (0.3 m) in diameter. It could carry a 25-pound (11 kg) package of instruments to an altitude of 100,000 feet (30,480 m). On its first flight, the rocket achieved an altitude of 45 miles (72 km), twice what its developers expected.

The development of the WAC-Corporal slowed when captured V-2 rockets became available. But the stock of V-2s was not unlimited. When only a few were left, Aerojet was asked to develop a replacement for the WAC-Corporal. The result was the Aerobee, which could carry a payload of 150 pounds (68 kg) to an altitude of more than 50 miles (80 km).

The Space Shuttle

Although most people do not think of it as such, the space shuttle is a launch vehicle. One of its purposes is to carry satellites and space probes into space. The space shuttle is a combination of different types of rockets working together.

The shuttle itself has liquid-fuel engines that burn liquid hydrogen and liquid oxygen. When the engines are running, all that comes out is superheated steam. If you look closely at a photo of a shuttle launch, you will see that it looks as though nothing is coming out of the shuttle's main engines. There is no smoke at all but only the faintest, bluish flame. That is because steam is an invisible gas.

Fuel and oxidizer for the shuttle's main engines are carried in a huge external tank attached to the underside of the shuttle. The space shuttle carries no fuel on board. As soon as it has used up the propellants in the tank, the tank is discarded. (This happens very quickly. If water, instead of fuel, were pumped by the

This photo, taken during the launch of a space shuttle, illustrates a major difference between two types of rocket motors. The two solid-fuel boosters attached to the sides of the large orange main tank produce an intense flame and thick clouds of smoke. The three main engines of the shuttle, however, produce only a bright glow and no visible flame at all. This is because the main engines burn hydrogen and oxygen. The only by-product of this combustion is water, so what you see coming from the main engines is nothing more than superheated steam.

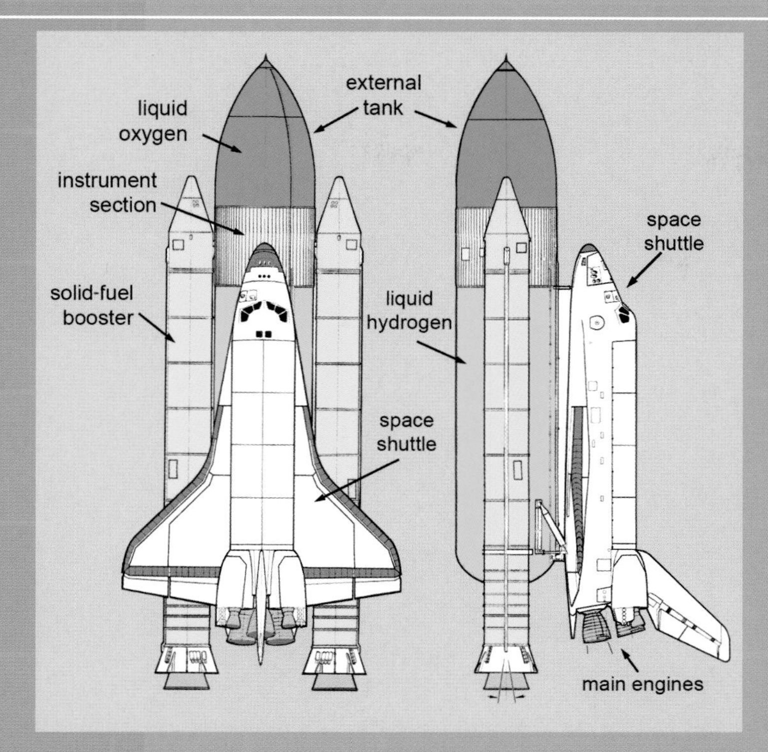

The space shuttle is a complex, multistage rocket. The shuttle itself carries no fuel or oxidizer. Instead, its main engines are supplied with liquid hydrogen and liquid oxygen from a huge external tank attached to the belly of the spacecraft. Two solid-fuel strap-on boosters are attached to the sides of the tank. These boosters are jettisoned as soon as their propellant is burned up. Once the external tank is empty, it, too, is discarded.

three main engines, an average family-sized swimming pool could be drained in twenty-five seconds). From then on, the shuttle carries no fuel. When it returns from space, it is an unpowered glider.

The big boosters strapped onto the sides of the shuttle are solid-fuel rockets. They are made of exotic materials, such as carbon fiber, and use modern fuel mixtures. But the solid-fuel boosters are not too different from the rockets that Congreve or Hale made nearly two hundred years ago. They are essentially enormous metal tubes packed with fuel. A central hollow core allows the fuel to burn evenly. And like a Congreve rocket, once the solid-fuel boosters are ignited, they can be neither turned off nor controlled. They will burn at full force until all of their fuel is spent.

NASA engineers test a solid-fuel booster for a space shuttle in the 1980s.

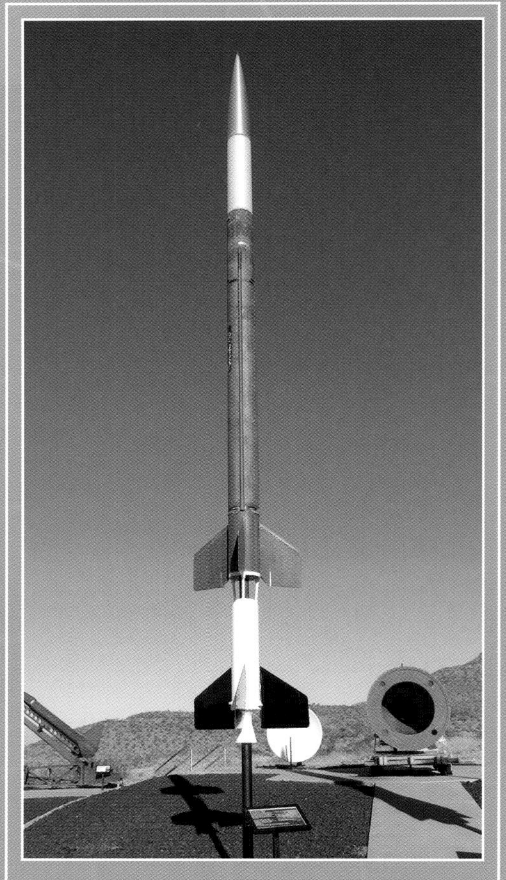

Aerobee sounding rockets are used to gather information about the upper atmosphere.

First launched in 1947, the Aerobee enjoyed a successful career of more than thirty-eight years. Meanwhile, the Aerobee carried a wide variety of instruments, adding immeasurably to our knowledge of the upper atmosphere. Aerobees carried some of the first living creatures—mice and small monkeys—to the edge of space. They also took the first color photographs of Earth from space and made numerous important astronomical observations and discoveries. The last Aerobee was launched in 1985.

The successor to the Aerobee was the Viking, developed by the U.S. Navy. Much larger than the Aerobee—at about 46 feet (14 m) long—the Viking was capable of reaching altitudes of more than 150 miles (241 km). The Viking boasted a large number of innovative features, not the least of which was its gimballed engine. Set into a pair of nested rings, the engine could be swung in any direction. Connected to an autopilot, this allowed the rocket to maintain a steady, stable, straight course. This rock-solid stability was extremely important when taking delicate scientific measurements, such as those involving individual stars, where a steady view is essential.

Unfortunately, large liquid-fuel rockets like the Viking are expensive. At $400,000 per launch (in 1950s dollars), the Viking simply cost too much to be used as a sounding rocket. This was a boon for the development of solid-fuel sounding rockets. One of the earliest developed after World War II was the Deacon, which was only 1 percent of the cost of a Viking to launch. With the help of a booster, the Deacon could carry a 50-pound (23 kg) payload to nearly 70 miles (113 km) above the surface of Earth. This allowed instruments to measure near-space conditions and make observations above the bulk of Earth's atmosphere. This success led to an entire family of low-cost, efficient solid-fuel sounding rockets that used existing rockets by "stacking" them.

Other countries also developed sounding rockets, both solid-fuel and liquid-fuel. The Soviets created a large number of them beginning in the 1950s. The French began launching the liquid-fuel

The most popular sounding rocket was the two-stage, solid-propellant Nike-Apache. Large numbers of Nike-Apache rockets were launched by NASA between 1962 and 1980.

Veronique in 1950. The Veronique had been developed, like so many others, from the V-2. It was so successful that it became the French equivalent of the American Aerobee. It was used for decades.

Britain did not develop a sounding rocket of its own until the mid-1950s. The liquid-fuel Skylark was designed by Walter Riedel, who had been von Braun's deputy at Peenemunde. More than 350 Skylarks were launched. Later models, such as the three-stage Skylark 12, carried 770-pound (350 kg) payloads as high as 620 miles (998 km).

Meanwhile, Japan developed tiny solid-fuel rockets, which were just 9 to 12 inches (23 to 30 cm) long and less than 1 inch (2.5 cm) in diameter. They were called pencil rockets because of their size and shape. These tiny rockets provided valuable data on propellants and engine design.

From the pencil rockets grew the Kappa series of liquid-fuel rockets. In 1958 a Kappa 6 carried a 6-pound (2.7 kg) payload to an altitude of 135 miles (217 km). Eventually the Japanese developed their successful Lambda series of four-stage solid-fuel sounding rockets. A Lambda rocket launched *Osumi*, Japan's first satellite.

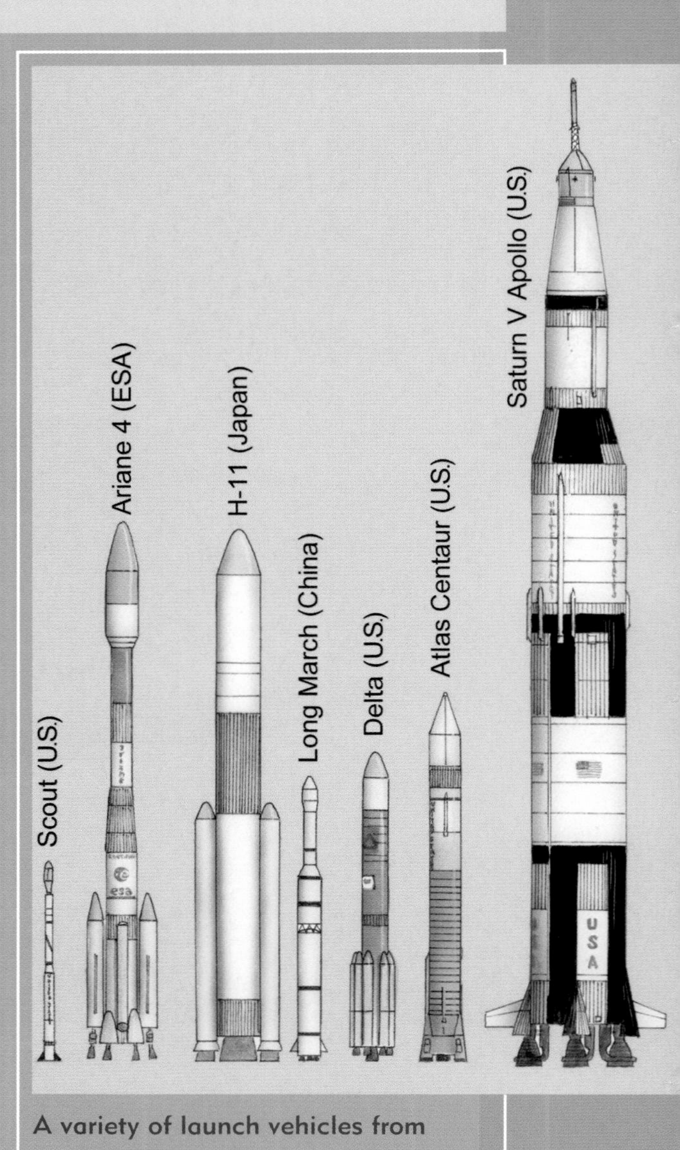

A variety of launch vehicles from around the world

Australia, India, Canada, Israel, and Brazil have also developed sounding rockets for scientific research. The simplicity and inexpensiveness of sounding rockets has enabled countries that do not have the facilities to develop rockets of their own to purchase them from other nations. This has given many small countries the ability to participate in important scientific research.

All Kinds of Rockets

Rockets are not limited to scientific research, space exploration, or the military. After the great ocean liner *Titanic* struck an iceberg in April 1912, its crew desperately tried to summon help by firing signal rockets. The ship carried thirty-six rockets to be used in an emergency. They were the most up-to-date maritime models. They were different from previous signal rockets because they carried an explosive device that created a loud bang in addition to a shower of white stars.

Unfortunately, the crew members who fired the rockets did not do so properly. The international distress signal required that a rocket be fired once every minute. Instead, the crew fired only eight rockets at irregular intervals over the period of one hour. This signaled only that the ship was having problems navigating. Thus, at least one potential rescue ship ignored *Titanic*'s cry for help.

One of the earliest civilian uses for rockets—other than for signaling—was for lifesaving. A lifesaving rocket was used by the British to rescue people from sinking ships. One end of a rope was fastened to a stronghold on the rescue vessel, while the other end was attached to a rocket. When the rescuers shot the rocket, the rope was propelled across the water and landed on the sinking ship. Passengers and crew could use the rope to make their way to safety.

Although Congreve designed one of the earliest lifesaving rockets, they were refined by other inventors such as John Dennett (1790–1852).

Dennett's rockets were fired from lightweight, portable stands that could be set up and aimed by anyone. Some of his rockets were designed to snag themselves in a ship's rigging or to attach themselves to parts of the wreck. This was in case the ship's crew was too exhausted to attach the line. Thousands of people have been saved using these rockets, and modern forms of lifesaving rockets are still used.

In the nineteenth century, whaling was an important and lucrative industry because oil from whale blubber was used to fuel lanterns. Whalers used rockets to shoot harpoons from the decks of small boats into the bodies of whales. Successful rocket attacks on whales were recorded as early as 1821. The captain of the *Fame* boasted that he had caught nine whales with rocket harpoons.

Years later, a whaling rocket was patented by Thomas Welcome Roys, a U.S. whaling captain, and Gustavus Adolphus Lilliendahl, a

When lifesaving rockets were used, a light line was carried by the rocket to the ship in distress.

Whalers once used rocket-powered harpoons to hunt the huge animals.

fireworks manufacturer from New York City. Thinking that the Roys-Lilliendahl rocket harpoon was not powerful enough, John Nelson Fletcher and Robert L. Suits designed their own rocket in 1878 and began selling it. The Fletcher-Suits rocket harpoon was 6.5 feet (2 m) long and weighed 32 pounds (15 kg). According to the manufacturers, it could hit a whale 180 feet (55 m) away. It was considerably more effective than a hand-thrown harpoon.

In modern times, rocket-propelled harpoons are rarely if ever used. Whalers instead use harpoons fired by high-powered guns. These are more accurate and don't have to be used at such dangerously close range to the whale as a rocket had to be.

Rockets are also good at making objects move fast. In the early 1950s, an air force doctor named John Paul Stapp was in an air force study of the effects of deceleration on the human body—or the effect

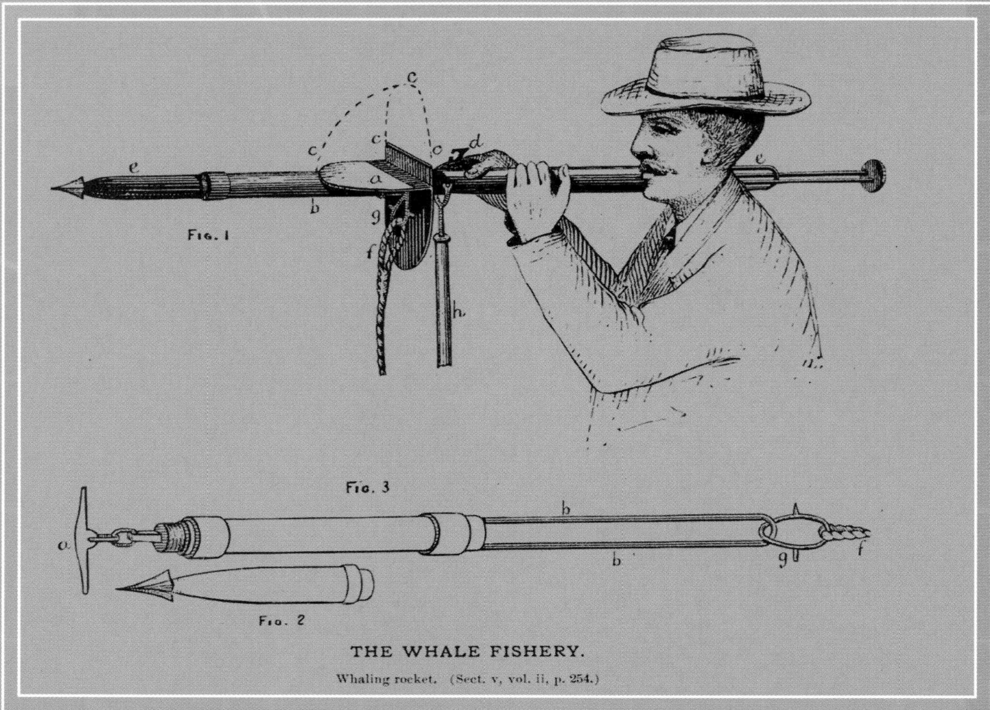

This illustration from a nineteenth-century U.S. manual shows the proper use of a rocket harpoon.

of coming to a sudden stop when traveling at a high speed. One goal was to increase survival rates in airplane crashes.

So a special rocket-powered sled—dubbed Sonic Wind I—that ran along a track in the New Mexico desert was built. On December 10, 1954, Dr. Stapp strapped himself into the seat. Twelve large solid-fuel motors accelerated him from a standing start to 632 miles (1,017 km) an hour in just five seconds. At the end of the track, scoops built into the bottom of the sled hit a reservoir of water between the tracks. The sled came to a complete stop in just 1.3 seconds.

This created a force on Dr. Stapp's body more than forty times that of gravity, increasing his weight to 6,800 pounds (3,087 kg) almost instantly. Not only did he set a land speed record, Stapp's work helped in developing seat belts and improving aircraft seats, restraints, and other safety devices. This has saved many lives.

Rocket-propelled sleds were used in the 1950s and 1960s to provide data relating to the effects of high acceleration and deceleration on the human body. *Top:* A rocket sled has been fitted with ten large solid-fuel motors. When these motors are ignited, the sled will race down the track at an extremely high speed. At the end of the run, a scoop on the bottom will hit a pool of water between the tracks, slowing the sled to a stop. *Second from top:* This rocket sled was used to test escape systems for fighter pilots. *Third from top:* A sled races down a track under full rocket power. *Bottom:* Using a combination of water and a parachute, an experimental rocket sled is brought to a halt.

Model Rocketry

Building and flying model rockets is an exciting hobby that has attracted tens of thousands of enthusiasts. The model rocket, as it has become known, was invented in 1954 by Orville Carlisle, a licensed pyrotechnics expert, and his brother Robert, a model airplane builder. They were inspired by a series of magazine articles written by the aerospace engineer G. Harry Stine.

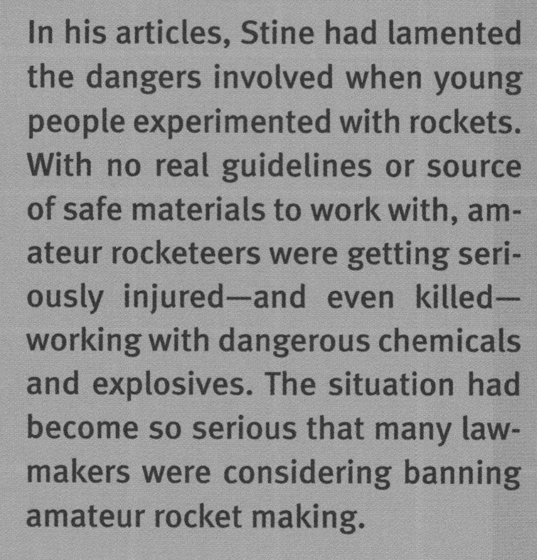

In his articles, Stine had lamented the dangers involved when young people experimented with rockets. With no real guidelines or source of safe materials to work with, amateur rocketeers were getting seriously injured—and even killed—working with dangerous chemicals and explosives. The situation had become so serious that many lawmakers were considering banning amateur rocket making.

Young rocketeers of the twenty-first century enjoy the safe launch of a model rocket along with former vice president Al Gore and former Minnesota governor Jesse Ventura.

Other scientists had experimented with using solid-fuel rockets to help boost the takeoff of heavy aircraft. This technique—later called JATO—was perfected during World War II. It helped aircraft that were either too heavy to get airborne on their own or had to take off from runways too short to allow them to accelerate enough. Although not used as often as they were a few decades ago, JATO units are still occasionally employed in special circumstances.

Carlisle realized that the answer lay in a series of commercially manufactured, standardized motors. These could then be used safely by the hobbyists in whatever rocket design they created. The motors would come in assorted sizes so rocket makers could pick the one that worked best for their rocket. Carlisle sent samples of these motors to Stine—who was then working as the range safety officer at the White Sands Missile Range in New Mexico—who tested them successfully. Stine eventually became not only an enthusiastic amateur rocketeer but one of the hobby's most enthusiastic promoters.

The typical rocket motor consists of a heavy paper cylinder. At one end is a clay nozzle, then the propellant, followed by a nonpropellant that burns but does not add any thrust. This is called the coast (or delay) phase. Finally, an ejection charge is used to deploy the rocket's parachute. Because of the excellence of the motor's design as well as the strict adherence of model rocketeers to safety rules, literally hundreds of millions of motors have been used in the past fifty years without serious accident.

The motor is, of course, only part of a model rocket. The rest consists of a tube—usually cardboard—that contains a mount for the engine, stabilizing fins, a parachute, and a nose cone. The rocket may also contain a payload. This might consist, for instance, of a small camera that will automatically snap a photo at the highest point of the rocket's flight.

Rockets also test the strength of containers meant to carry hazardous nuclear wastes. The U.S. Department of Energy smashes these containers with every type of vehicle available. To get these vehicles going fast enough to simulate a real wreck, they are often accelerated by rockets. Full-size locomotive engines have even been accelerated with rockets, sending them hurtling down the tracks to collide with a truck carrying an empty nuclear waste container. A

The National Association of Rocketry

In 1957, the same year that Carlisle and Stine developed the safe amateur rocket, the National Association of Rocketry (NAR) was formed. Among many other things, the NAR organizes clubs, rocketry meets, contests, and competitions. It also advocates the safe use of model rockets. As part of this program, it established a safety code that all amateur rocket makers must promise to abide by. The NAR and its code are largely responsible for the hobby being one of the safest in the world. You can find the NAR safety code at http://nar.org/NARmrsc.html.

rocket-powered locomotive is an impressive thing to see!

Perhaps the ultimate in rocket travel is a rocket-propelled human being. The rocket backpack—or Small Rocket Lift Device (SRLD)—was developed by Bell Aerosystems for the U.S. Army. It was tested in 1961. The idea was to create a small personal propulsion device that would be strapped to the back of a soldier. It would enable soldiers to use low-power rocket propulsion to rapidly but safely travel or leap over short distances like small rivers or ravines and land upright on their feet. Unfortunately, the 125-pound (56 kg) weight of the SRLD, combined with a flight time of only twenty-six seconds, made it too limited for practical use.

Rockets in World Culture

In addition to the role they play in space exploration, scientific research, and the military, rockets are also an important part of many cultures around the world. Traditional Fourth of July skyrockets have been a familiar part of Independence Day celebrations for nearly two hundred years. They serve to remind Americans of the rockets that fell on Fort McHenry during the War of 1812.

In Mexico many saint's days are celebrated with fireworks and rockets. Of course, Chinese New Year wouldn't be complete without rockets, especially in the culture that had originally invented them. Perhaps the most extraordinary cultural use of rockets is the enormous festival rockets of Japan and Southeast Asia. In Thailand and Laos, they are called Boun Bang Fai rockets, meaning "the merit of firing rockets." They have deep roots in Buddhist and traditional symbolism.

These rockets, built and launched for perhaps as long as one thousand years, are enormous constructions. They are hand made from bamboo and paper and lavishly decorated with colored foil, banners, garlands, tassels, and dragon heads. They may be as large as 6.5 to 13 feet (2 to 4 m) long with bamboo guide sticks up to 45 feet (13.7 m) long. Filled with up to several hundred pounds of gunpowder, these beautiful rockets rise 300 to 500 feet (90 to 150 m) into the sky.

Southeast Asian festival rockets are hand made by villagers using techniques unchanged for hundreds of years. These giant rockets are launched during special religious festivals such as this one in Thailand.

7 THE FUTURE OF ROCKETS

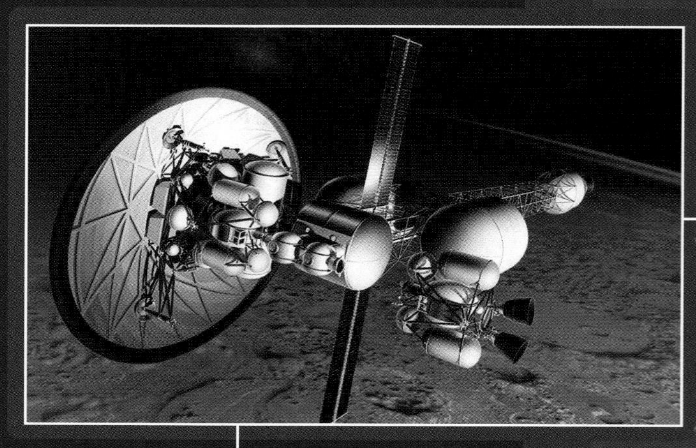

All rockets work through the principle of action-reaction. Something is ejected at high speed from one end, causing the rocket to move in the opposite direction. This "something" in the rockets we've described so far has been a hot gas, produced by burning fuels. But it does not have to be a hot gas. Whatever is being ejected must be done so at a very high speed. When you blow up a balloon and release it, it will fly around the room like a rocket because of the reaction to the air it is expelling—and that air is not even hot, let alone burning.

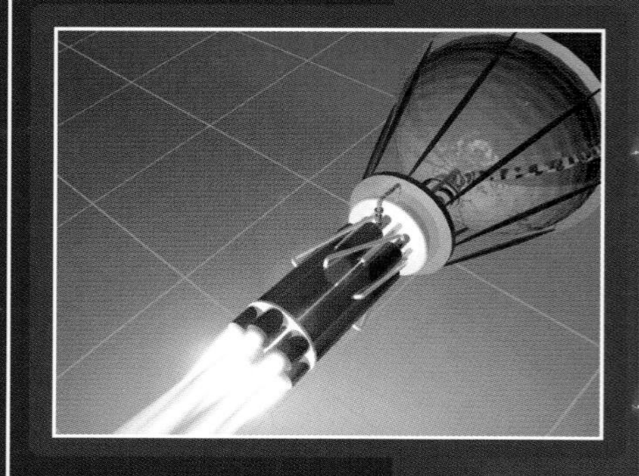

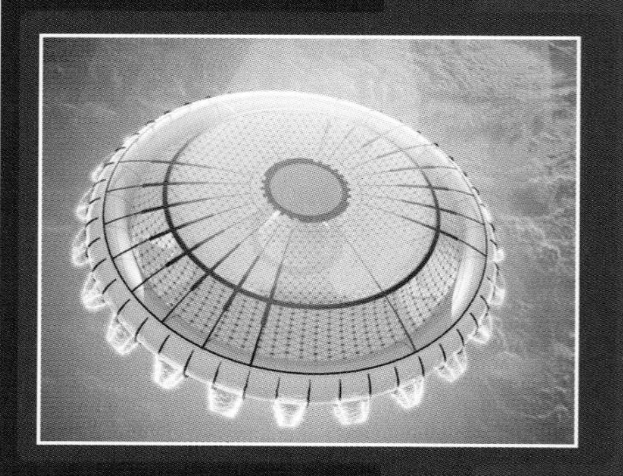

Modern engineers work on rocket systems that Goddard and von Braun would have never dreamed of. Nuclear-thermal rockets *(top)* may take explorers to Mars. The Pulse Detonation System *(middle)* is a chemical-fueled descendant of the Orion Project. Rockets may even be powered by microwaves instead of hot gases from burning fuels *(bottom)*.

Back in the 1920s, several scientists, including Hermann Oberth, suggested that matter could be ejected at high speed by electricity. Ionic air filters are a good example of how electric rockets work. Two metal plates are given opposite electrical charges. Air is drawn into one side of the filter and given a positive charge by one of the metal plates. It is then repelled by the positive charge of the second plate, since similar electrical charges repel one another. This creates a stream of air flowing through the filter. This same effect can create a stream of gas flowing from the engine of a rocket. Electric rocket engines are often called ion thrusters because an atom with an electrical charge is called an ion.

There have been many different plans for ion rockets since the 1920s, but all work more or less on the same principle. First, a gas is given an electrical charge. Then it is propelled from the nozzle of the rocket by passing it through a grid bearing the same electrical charge as the gas. Engines such as this produce low thrusts, but they also require little fuel. It almost seems as though they can run nonstop indefinitely. So although an ion rocket starts off slowly, its exhaust eventually builds up to tremendous speeds. The actual thrust, however, is very low, so ion engines can be used only in space and not to launch spacecraft from Earth.

Ion engines have been successfully tested in space. They have been used on satellites as efficient, low-thrust engines for adjusting the position of the spacecraft. An ion engine was used on a Japanese space probe that made a historic touchdown on an asteroid in 2005. The *Hayabusa* spacecraft, using the gentle nudges from a NASA-developed ion engine, scooped up samples of the surface of asteroid Itokawa for eventual return to Earth. A soil sample from an asteroid will yield clues about the raw materials that made up the planets and asteroids in their formative years. Even the smallest sample from an asteroid can have huge scientific value.

Electric Propulsion

If you rub a balloon against a wool sweater, you will cause atoms on the surface of the balloon to exchange electrons with atoms in the sweater. These atoms then become ions, or atoms with either too many or too few electrons. You can tell that the balloon has been charged with ions (or static electricity) because its negatively charged atoms will be attracted to the positively charged atoms of your body. The balloon will stick to you.

Ion engines work in a similar way. Instead of having ions that are simply attracted to one another, ion engines pull ions past plates with opposite charges and out the back of the engine. The ejection of the ions creates thrust, just as the ejection of gases in a regular rocket engine does.

The ion engine consists of an ionization device called a cathode. The cathode sends electrons into the propellant. The electrons hit the propellant atoms and remove one or more of their electrons. These atoms have become positive ions. A positively charged plate in the front of the engine pushes these atoms forward. A negatively charged grid in the back of the engine pulls these ions out at great speeds. Just outside the last plate is another cathode that neutralizes the ion beam. Otherwise, it would be attracted right back toward the rocket.

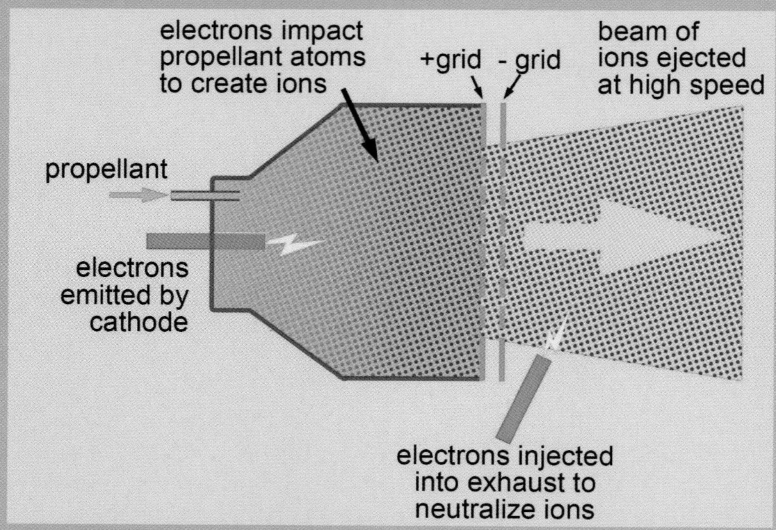

In an ion motor, a beam of ionized particles replaces the hot gases of a conventional rocket motor.

DEEP SPACE 1

NASA's *Deep Space 1* space probe was launched on October 24, 1998. During a highly successful primary mission, it tested twelve advanced technologies in space, including ion propulsion. The spacecraft's ion engine provided about ten times the specific impulse (ratio of thrust to propellant used) of an ordinary liquid-fuel engine. As an extension of its original mission, *Deep Space 1* encountered the asteroid Braille and the comet Borrelly. It returned the best images and other data ever obtained from a comet.

The *Deep Space 1* spacecraft used its ion engine to maneuver close enough to Comet Borrelly to obtain detailed photographs of its surface.

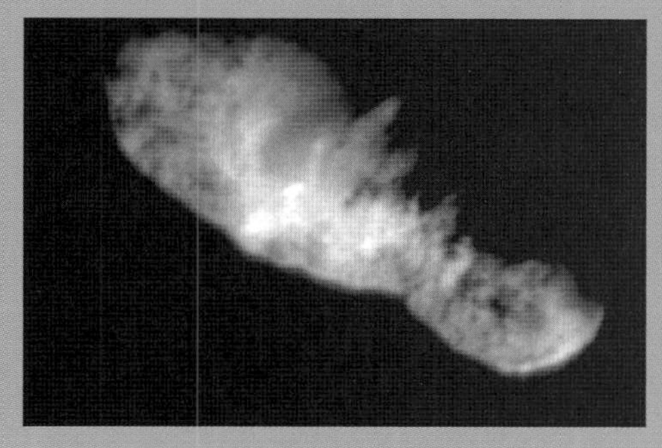

This is the highest resolution photo of the comet that was obtained by *Deep Space 1*.

Electricity, generated by nuclear power perhaps, could also make a fluid hot enough to vaporize. This is the same way that the electric element on a kitchen range can turn the water in a teakettle into steam. The "steam" from such a rocket—which may be at a temperature of thousands of degrees—can be used to propel it.

Scientists at NASA's Marshall Space Flight Center in Alabama have been working on several unusual forms of rocket propulsion. One obtains its energy from nuclear fusion. Unlike fission, in which an atom is split to release energy, fusion combines two or more atoms to create a heavier atom. It releases tremendous amounts of energy in the process—energy that could propel a spaceship. The creation of fusion

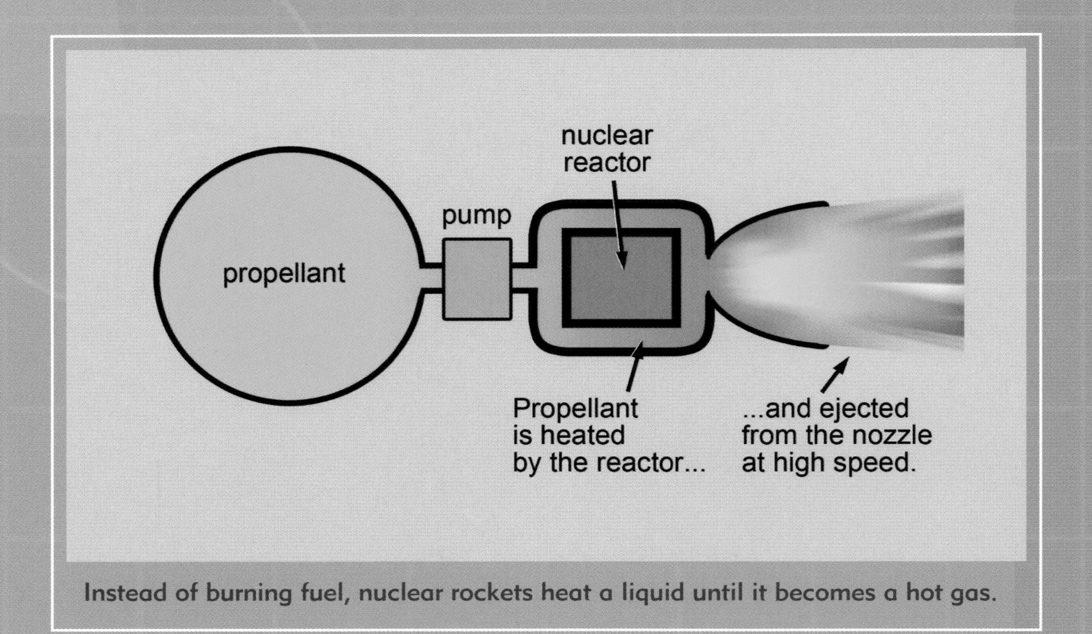

Instead of burning fuel, nuclear rockets heat a liquid until it becomes a hot gas.

energy is so efficient that it would be like driving a car 7,000 miles (11,265 km) on a single gallon (3.8 liters) of gas. This energy could create power for an ion thruster. Also, the superhot plasma created by fusion could be ejected from a nozzle to propel the spaceship directly.

Another exotic source of energy is from antimatter. Antimatter is identical to normal matter, except that the electrical charges of its atomic particles are reversed. A normal proton is positive where an antiproton is negative. When normal matter and antimatter meet, they annihilate each other in a huge burst of energy. If this energy were to be channeled out the back end of a spaceship, it could produce thrust. Although scientists believe that antimatter may exist freely in the universe somewhere, the only samples so far have been produced in laboratories.

The beauty of matter/antimatter propulsion would be that a tiny amount of matter would produce a vast amount of energy. An antimatter-propelled spaceship could attain huge speeds while having to carry very little fuel. Of course, the main problem facing engineers working with antimatter is how to store a substance that explodes instantly the moment it touches anything.

Other unique rockets use conventional fuels but with radically redesigned engines. The plug nozzle, or aerospike engine, for example, is nothing more than a conventional rocket engine turned wrong side out. The flow of gases from the burning fuel clings to the outside of the curved nozzle. The advantage to the plug nozzle is that an engine can be much shorter than a conventional one. The savings in weight means the rocket can carry more fuel.

Other engineers have concentrated on ordinary rockets that use extraordinary fuels. Different fuels may be more powerful or less expensive to make or safer to store. For example, *SpaceShipOne*, the

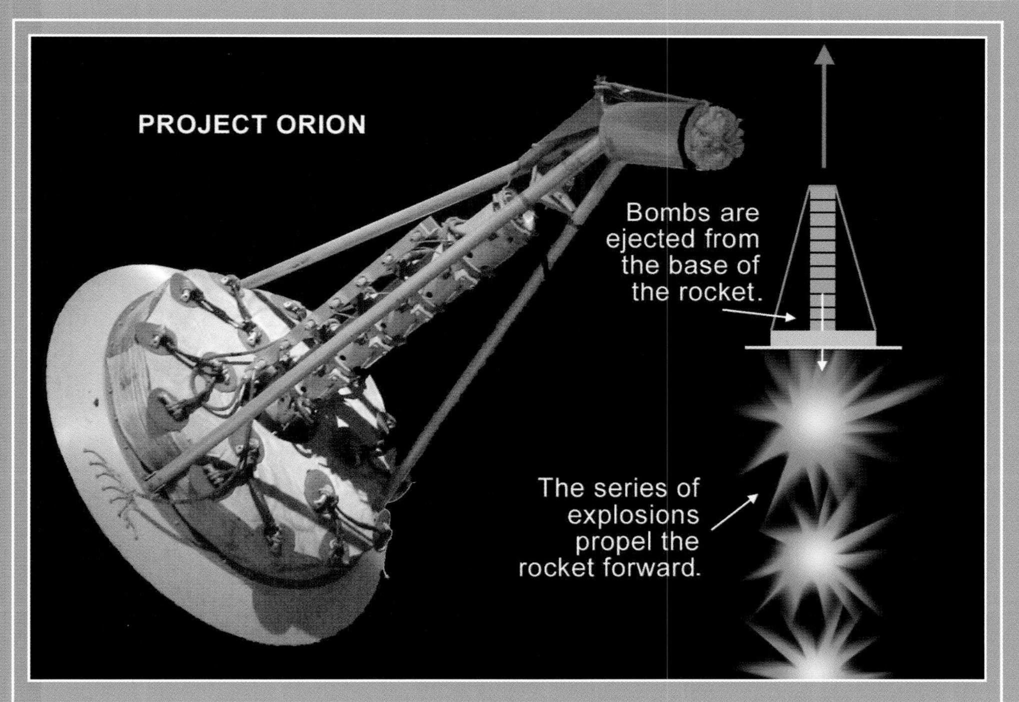

One of the most unusual reaction-propelled spacecraft ever suggested was Project Orion. A series of nuclear bombs were to be ejected through a hole in a huge steel plate. When the bombs detonated, they would force the spacecraft forward. A model *(left)* was tested by NASA and the Atomic Energy Commission using conventional explosives. But international treaties regarding aboveground nuclear testing, as well as fears about radioactive pollution, put a stop to the project before full-scale testing could begin.

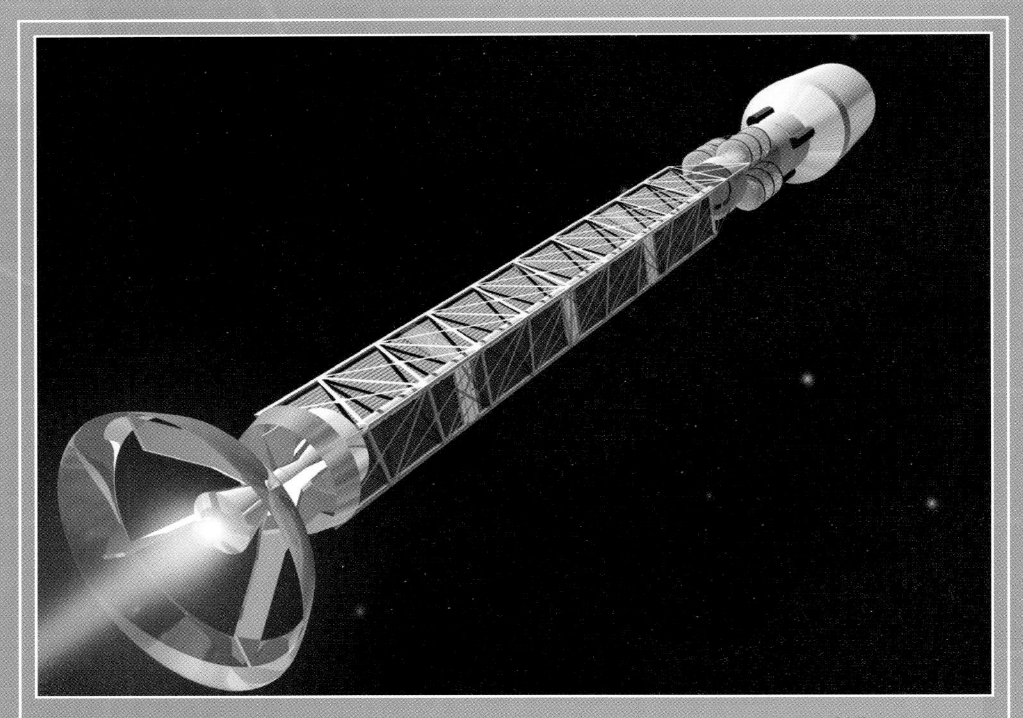

Scientists think that future spacecraft may have antimatter engines. When matter and antimatter particles are combined, they mutually annihilate one another in a tremendous burst of energy—about 10 billion times more powerful than the energy released by ordinary rocket fuels. Such spacecraft are still many years in the future, however. The main problem is that antimatter doesn't exist in nature. It has to be manufactured. So far, scientists have only been able to create a few particles of antimatter. Also, scientists would have to find a way to store a substance that can't be allowed to come into contact with ordinary matter.

first private spaceship ever developed—which made its first flight into space in 2004—employed a rocket motor that burned solid fuel with a liquid oxidizer. The fuel was made of rubber processed from old automobile tires. The oxidizer was nitrous oxide, best known as an anesthetic used by doctors. A rocket engine that uses a solid fuel and a liquid or gaseous oxidizer is called a hybrid rocket. Unlike ordinary solid-fuel motors, such as those that boost the space shuttle, an engine like *SpaceShipOne*'s can be turned on and off. (Some new solid-fuel motors can be turned on and off at will.)

Hybrid Fuels and the Candlestick Rocket

In their search for new rocket fuels, scientists have tried many unusual materials. A recent discovery, however, is one of the most ordinary materials imaginable: candle wax. Scientists figured out a way to make candle wax—or paraffin—burn fast enough to serve as rocket fuel. Unlike the candles on a birthday cake, however, this paraffin burns in the presence of pure oxygen gas. This causes it to burn much hotter and faster.

One of the exciting things about this discovery is that paraffin rocket fuel would be much simpler and safer to work with than the toxic, explosive fuels. An ordinary household candle can be safely carved, melted, and molded. If free from artificial colors or perfumes, it can even be chewed on. In contrast, solid-fuel rockets use materials in which the fuel and oxidizer are mixed together before being packed into the rocket. So the fuel is ready to explode—an unsafe material to work with, as well as environmentally unfriendly.

When ordinary solid fuels burn, they produce many noxious chemicals. When it rains, these compounds find their way into lakes and soils where they can harm plant and animal life. Paraffin, in contrast, burns cleanly. The only gases left behind are water vapor and carbon dioxide.

The other advantage to hybrid fuels such as paraffin—where a solid fuel is combined with a liquid oxidizer—is that they allow for controllable rockets. They can be turned on and off just by turning on and off the flow of oxidizer. Their thrust can be throttled the same way.

Many other unusual rockets are either on the drawing board or are being tested. Some of these are based on existing principles and materials, while others have to wait for the development of future technologies—which may or may not come to pass. Either way, the rockets of this century will look as primitive and quaint to future space explorers as Fourth of July skyrockets look to us now.

Want to Be a Rocket Scientist?

Do you enjoy math and science? Do you have an inquisitive and searching mind? Are you interested in knowing what makes things work? Do you like to solve problems and puzzles? Do you like to create things? Do you enjoy learning? Do you enjoy working with computers? Are you prepared to study hard and do homework? Do you get good grades? These are the questions that NASA asks of students who are interested in working in space science and engineering.

A career in aerospace can be exciting. People in the field are professionals who either work independently or as part of a team. They conduct research and design and develop vehicles and systems for atmospheric and space environments. Individuals who are successful in aerospace careers have the proper educational background, possess good communication skills, and are committed to being part of a team.

If you are interested in this field, consider taking mathematics and science. Courses such as algebra, geometry, trigonometry, calculus, and computer math are important, as are sciences such as biology, chemistry, and physics. English is important too, since ideas need to be understood and communicated accurately.

A high school curriculum that includes these subjects will prepare you for the four to seven years of college study following high school. A bachelor's degree is the minimum necessary to enter this field. Colleges and universities also offer graduate programs. The master's program usually takes two years. It takes an additional two to four years to earn a doctorate.

A starting position as an engineer, mathematician, physical scientist, or life scientist usually requires a bachelor's degree. (NASA prefers those working in the life sciences to have at least a master's and/or doctoral degree.) Some examples of engineering degrees required for aerospace technology are electrical/electronics, aerospace, and mechanical. Other types of bachelor's degrees that may lead to aerospace careers are physics, chemistry, geology, meteorology, mathematics, experimental psychology, and biology.

Engineering technicians typically have two-year associate of science degrees. Some will continue for an additional two years to obtain a bachelor's degree in engineering technology. Others earn bachelor's degrees in engineering or one of the physical sciences. Some technicians may complete one of the five-year apprenticeship programs offered at NASA field centers.

Once you have received this education, what can you do with it? What kinds of jobs or careers are in the aerospace industry? Probably a lot more than you think. The majority of jobs in aerospace fall into three broad categories: engineers, technicians, and scientists.

Engineers make things work. The work and ideas of engineers make achievements possible. They put power and materials to work. Rockets, spacecraft, and satellites are designed and built by various kinds of engineers. These include chemical, electrical, computer, nuclear, safety, and biomedical engineers, and many others. In the future, engineers will design safer and more efficient spacecraft, space stations, and space colonies.

Technicians are an important part of the aerospace team. They work closely with scientists and engineers. They operate wind tunnels, work in laboratories, construct test equipment, build models, and support many types of research. Technicians and designers are always in demand. The industry also needs writers, artists, and photographers.

Scientists are knowledge seekers, always searching out why things happen. They are inquisitive. They possess a sense of wonder. Nature, Earth, and the universe fascinate the scientist. The scientist asks questions, seeks answers, and expands knowledge. You could be an astronomer, chemist, geologist, physicist, or meteorologist. If you are more interested in the life sciences, biologists, medical doctors, psychologists, and other scientists are needed. Or a degree in math may lead you to become a systems analyst or computer scientist. And you could, of course, be an astronaut, working as a pilot, mission specialist, or payload specialist.

Glossary

alchemist: a person who attempted to turn base metals into gold. Alchemists prior to the seventeenth century paved the way for the development of the science of chemistry.

antimatter: matter consisting of elementary particles that are the antiparticles of those making up normal matter. When antimatter is combined with an equal amount of ordinary matter, the result is the complete and direct conversion of both into energy.

atom: the smallest unit of an element, having all the characteristics of that element

bazooka: a military device consisting of a hollow metal tube that a soldier can use to safely launch a specially made rocket

cathode: a negatively charged electrode, as of an electrolytic cell, a storage battery, or an electron tube

centrifugal force: not actually a "force" at all but rather an apparent force that makes a body move away from its center of rotation. It is caused by the inertia of the body.

combustion chamber: the part of the rocket motor where the fuel and oxidizer are combined and burned

electron: a stable subatomic particle with a negative electrical charge

fission: a nuclear reaction in which an atomic nucleus splits into fragments and releases energy

fusion: a nuclear reaction in which atomic nuclei combine to form more massive nuclei with the simultaneous release of energy

inert gas: a gas, such as neon or helium, that does not readily combine with any other element

ion: an atom or a group of atoms that has acquired an electrical charge by gaining or losing one or more electrons

ion thruster: a type of rocket that uses a beam of ions to create thrust

JATO: acronym for jet-assisted takeoff

launch vehicles: rockets used to boost satellites or other spacecraft

mass ratio: the weight of the fully fueled rocket compared to its empty weight

matter: something that has mass and exists as a solid, liquid, gas, or plasma

molecule: a combination of two or more atoms. Water, for example, is a molecule made up of two atoms of hydrogen and one of oxygen

oxidizer: the source of oxygen used to burn fuel

payload: the explosive charge carried in the warhead of a missile; the cargo of a rocket, such as an instrument package

propellant: the material that is burned in a rocket motor; the material that is ejected from the nozzle to provide reaction

recoil: the backward action of a firearm or rocket

regenerative cooling: using the rocket's own fuel to cool its motor

thrust: the forward-directed force developed in a rocket engine as a reaction to the high-velocity rearward ejection of exhaust gases

velocity: the rate at which an object is moving

Source Notes

8 Jixing Pan, *On the Origin of Rockets* (Beijing: Institute for the History of Science, Chinese Academy of Science, 1984), 177.

9 Ibid., 174.

15 Willy Ley, *Rockets, Missiles and Men in Space* (New York: Signet Books, 1968), 88.

34 Milton Lehman, *Robert H. Goddard: Pioneer of Space Research* (New York: Da Capo Press, 1988), 111.

53 Ley, 176.

54 Frank Winter, *Rockets into Space* (Cambridge, MA: Harvard University Press, 1990), 46.

58–59 Lehman, 301.

62 Winter, 46.

65 Ibid., 52.

Bibliography

Gatland, Kenneth. *The Illustrated Encyclopedia of Space Technology*. London: Orion Books, 1989.

Ley, Willy. *Rockets, Missiles, and Men in Space*. New York: Signet Books, 1968.

Ordway, Frederick I., and Wernher von Braun. *The Rockets' Red Glare*. Nelson, NZ: Anchor Press, 1976.

———. *Space Travel: A History*. New York: Harper & Row, 1985.

Reynolds, David. *Apollo: The Epic Journey to the Moon*. New York: Harcourt, 2002.

Winter, Frank. *The First Golden Age of Rocketry*. Washington, DC: Smithsonian Institution Press, 1990.

———. *Rockets into Space*. Cambridge, MA: Harvard University Press, 1990.

For Further Information

Books

Clary, David A. *Rocket Man: Robert H. Goddard and the Birth of the Space Age*. New York: Theia Books, 2004.

Crouch, Tom D. *Aiming for the Stars: The Dreamers and Doers of the Space Age*. Washington, DC: Smithsonian Institution Scholarly Press, 2000.

Dyson, George. *Project Orion: The True Story of the Atomic Spaceship*. New York: Henry Holt, 2002.

Hickam, Homer. *Rocket Boys*. New York: Delacorte Press, 2000.

Kuhn, Betsy. *The Race for Space: The United States and the Soviet Union Compete for the New Fronteir.* Minneapolis: Twenty-First Century Books, 2007.

Sherman, Josepha. *The Cold War*. Minneapolis: Twenty-First Century Books, 2004.

Streissguth, Tom. *Rocket Man: The Story of Robert Goddard*. Minneapolis: Twenty-First Century Books, 1995.

Ward, Bob. *Dr. Space: The Life of Wernher von Braun*. Annapolis, MD: Naval Institute Press, 2005.

Museums

Kansas Cosmosphere and Space Center
1100 N. Plum
Hutchinson, KS 67501
http://www.cosmo.org/visitorinfo/whyhutch.php

Kennedy Space Center
State Road 405
Kennedy Space Center, FL 32899
http://www.kennedyspacecenter.com

Pima Air & Space Museum
6000 E. Valencia Rd.
Tucson, AZ 85706
http://www.pimaair.org/

San Diego Air & Space Museum
2001 Pan American Plaza
Balboa Park, San Diego, CA 92101
http://www.aerospacemuseum.org/

Smithsonian National Air & Space Museum
6th & Independence SW
Washington, DC 20560
http://www.nasm.si.edu/

U.S. Space and Rocket Center
One Tranquility Base
Huntsville, AL 35805
http://www.spacecamp.com/museum/

Websites

Amateur Rocketry Society of America
http://www.space-rockets.com/arsa.html
This site gives a history of amateur rocketry and links to local groups.

HobbySpace—Rocketry
http://www.hobbyspace.com/Rocketry/index.html
This site provides discussions about model rocketry, high power rocketry, and advanced rocketry, as well as rocketry history, groups, contests, and up-to-date news.

NASA Home Page
http://www.nasa.gov
The official website of the National Aeronautics and Space Administration provides current mission photos and news.

NASA Jet Propulsion Laboratory
http://www.jpl.nasa.gov
The official JPL website provides lists of upcoming events and current research.

National Association of Rocketry
http://nar.org/index.html
This site provides the latest NAR rocketry news and displays local clubs and safety information.

Students for the Exploration and Development of Space
http://www.seds.org
This student-based organization promotes the exploration and development of space with programs, publications, membership, and discussion forums.

Index

A-1 rocket, 57
A-2 rocket, 57
A-3 rocket, 57, 60
A-4 rocket, 60, 62–63
action-reaction principle, 19–21, 22–23
Aerobee rocket, 72, 79–82
Aerojet, 79
aerospace careers, 102–103
aircraft, rocket-powered, 49
Ali, Hydar, 16
Ariane rocket, 78, 84
Army Ballistic Missile Agency, 68
Atlas ICBM, 71, 72–73, 84

Bacon, Roger, 12
Becker, Karl, 54
Braun, Wernher von, 42, 46, 51, 52, 54–63

cannons, 14, 19
careers, in aerospace field, 102–103
Carlisle, Orville and Robert, 90–91
cars, rocket-powered, 48
Chinese rocketry, 6–12
Ch'ing Hau-Tzu, 7
Coggins, Jack, 5, 10
Congreve, William, 17–18, 85
Congreve rockets, 16–19, 24, 27

Deacon rocket, 83
Deep Space 1, 97
Delta rockets, 73–75, 84
Dennett, John, 85–86
Die Rakete zu den Planetenräumen (book), 44
Dornberger, Walter, 53–54

Echo 1 satellite, 73–74
Eichstädtt, Konrad Kyeser von, 12
electric rockets, 95–97
Englebrunner von Horstig, D'Aubigny von, 54
Europa 1, 78
European Launcher Development Organization (ELDO), 78
European Space Agency (ESA), 78
European Space Research Organization, 78
Explorer 1 satellite, 69

festival rockets, 93
fire arrows, 8, 9, 11
fire lances, 9
fireworks, 7–9
Fletcher, John Nelson, 87
Fontana, Joanes de, 12–13
Fort McHenry, 24–25
French rocketry, 83–84
Froissart, Jean, 13
fuels: electric rockets, 95–97; liquid-fuel rockets, 35–37, 40–44, 50–52, 57; nuclear fusion, 97–98; nuclear-thermal rockets, 94; paraffin rocket fuel, 101; recent innovations, 100–101; solid-fuel rockets, 30–33, 40–41; solid fuel vs. liquid fuel, 40–41; space shuttle, 80–81

Geissler, Christoph Friedrich von, 14
Gemini program, 73
German rocketry. *See* Braun, Werner von; Verein für Raumshiffarht (VfR)
Gloria (mail plane), 70
Goddard, Robert, 30, 33–39, 56, 58–59, 64
Great Britain rocketry: in India, 16–19; sounding rockets, 84; War of 1812, 24–25
guidance and stability, 26–28, 60–61
gunpowder, 7, 12, 31
gyroscopic steering, 60–61

H-11 rocket, 84
Hale, William, 27
Hale rockets, 27–29
harpoon rockets, 86–88
Hayabusa spacecraft, 95
huo yao (fire drug), 7

India, 16–19
intercontinental ballistic missiles (ICBMs), 70
invention of rockets, 8, 9–12
ion rockets, 95–96
Italian rocketry, 12

Japanese rocketry, 84
JATO (jet-assisted takeoff), 65, 90
Jet Propulsion Laboratory, 79
Juno satellite launch vehicle, 68, 72
Jupiter-C rocket, 68, 69, 72

Kai-fung-fu, China, 9–11, 10
Key, Francis Scott, 24–25

launch vehicles, 71–78

Ley, Willy, 45, 46
lifesaving rockets, 85–86
Lilliendahl, Gustavus Adolphus, 86–87
Lindbergh, Charles A., 58
liquid-fuel rockets, 35–37, 40–41, 43–44, 52, 57

matter/antimatter rockets, 98–99, 100
Mercury Redstone, 72
military uses, of rockets: by British in India, 16–19; early uses, 12–15; War of 1812, 24–25; World War II, 54–63
Mirak (rocket), 51
Mirak III (rocket), 53
model rocketry, 90–92
multistage rockets, 67

National Association of Rocketry (NAR), 92
Nebel, Rudolf, 51–52, 54–55
Newton's laws of motion, 19–21
Nike-Apache rocket, 83
nuclear fusion, 97–98
nuclear-thermal rockets, 94

Oberth, Hermann, 42–45, 46, 95
Opel, Fritz von, 49
Osumi satellite, 84

Pioneer 3 satellite, 68
Project Bumper, 66, 72
Project Orion, 99
Propulsion, rocket: alternative vehicles, 48–49; electric rockets, 95–97; matter/antimatter rockets, 98–99, 100; microwaves, 94; nuclear fusion, 97–98; nuclear-thermal rockets, 94; principles of, 22–23; Pulse Detonation System, 94; and space travel, 29, 34–35
Pulse Detonation System, 94

R-7 rocket, 77
Rammah, Hassan al-, 11–12
recoil, 19–21
Redstone missile, 68
Reidel, Klaus, 51
Repulsor II (rocket), 53
rocket arrows, 9–11, 10
rocket harpoons, 86–88
The Rocket into Planetary Space (book), 44
rocket sleds, 88–89
Roys, Thomas Welcome, 86–87

safety research, 88–92
saltpeter, 6–7
satellites, 5, 72–78
Saturn V rocket, 76–77, 84
Scout rocket, 75, 84
Small Rocket Lift Device (SRLD), 92
Society for Space Travel. *See* Verein für Raumshiffarht (VfR)
solid-fuel rockets, 30–33, 40–41
Sonic Wind I, 88
sounding rockets, 79–85
Soviet Union rocketry, 68–70, 83
SpaceShipOne, 100
space shuttle, 80–81
space travel: Goddard's rockets, 33–39; Oberth's theories, 42–46; Tsiolkovsky's theories, 30–33; U.S. space program, 76–77, 80–81; Verne's writings, 28–29
steering rockets. *See* guidance and stability

thrust, 26
Tipu, Fateh Ali, 16–17
Titan ICBM, 71, 73
Tsiolkovsky, Konstantin E., 30–33

U.S. national anthem, 24–25
U.S. rocketry: Civil War, 28–29; naval rocketry, 70–71; post-World War II, 65–69; satellite launching, 72–78; space program, 76–77, 80–81; War of 1812, 24–25; World War II, 64–65. *See also* Goddard, Robert

V-2 rocket, 55, 56, 62–65
Valier, Max, 44, 48–49
Vanguard rocket, 72
Vehicle Assembly Building (VAB), 77
Verein für Raumshiffarht (VfR): early experiments, 50–54; founding of, 45–50; and German military, 54–63
Verne, Jules, 28–29, 42
Veronique rocket, 84
Viking rocket, 71, 72, 82–83

WAC-Corporal rocket, 66–68, 79
War of 1812, 24–25
White Sands Proving Grounds, 65–66
Winkler, Johannes, 47, 50–51
World War II, 62–63

About the Author

Ron Miller is the author and illustrator of about forty books, most of which have been about science, space, and astronomy. His award-winning books include *The Grand Tour* and *The History of Earth*. Among his nonfiction books for young people are *Special Effects, The Elements*, and the Worlds Beyond series, which received the 2003 American Institute of Physics Award in Physics and Astronomy. His book, *The Art of Chesley Bonestell*, won the 2002 Hugo Award for Best Non-Fiction. He has also designed space-themed postage stamps and has worked as an illustrator on several science fiction movies, such as *Dune* and *Total Recall*.

Photo Acknowledgments

All images were provided by the author except p. 90 (© Craig Lassig/AFP/ Getty Images).
Cover: © Bettmann/CORBIS